To

_____

From

_____

Date

_____

100 Days of Less Hustle, More Jesus: A Devotional Journal
Copyright © 2019 DaySpring Cards, Inc. All rights reserved
Artwork © 2019 Shanna Noel. Used by permission.
First Edition, May 2019

Published by:

P.O. Box 1010
Siloam Springs, AR 72761
dayspring.com

Written by: Paige DeRuyscher

Typeset Design by: Jessica Wei

Made in China

Prime: 89877

ISBN: 978-1-68408-605-4

100

days of

LESS HUSTLE, MORE JESUS

A Devotional Journal

SHANNA NOEL

HOME TO YOUR HEART

Guess what? You don't need an invitation to rest. You don't need someone to give you permission, and you don't have to prove that you deserve it. You. Are. Worthy. Always. Not just on the days when you feel like you've done enough or finally gotten things right. You are worthy because you are divinely created and infinitely loved. Can you hear that still, small voice calling you home to your heart? Jesus knows that the deepest love and the greatest transformation begin at His feet. Find your way there, as often as you can. He delights in your presence and longs to give you rest.

My beloved spoke and said to me,
"Arise, my darling, my beautiful one, come with me."
Song of Solomon 2:10 NIV

She had a sister called Mary,
who sat at the Lord's feet listening to what He said.
Luke 10:39 NIV

God decided in advance to adopt us into His own family
by bringing us to Himself through Jesus Christ.
This is what He wanted to do,
and it gave Him great pleasure.
Ephesians 1:5 NLT

For He Himself is our peace.

Ephesians 2:14 NIV

Jesus, remind me every day to rest in You, no matter what I'm doing
or how busy I think I am. I need time in Your presence more than
anything in the world. Thank You for calling me home to Your heart.

TAKE CARE OF YOU

When it comes to self-care, you've probably heard some version of "No one can pour from an empty cup." And yet the world would have you believe that you can and somehow should! Less sleep, more caffeine, more gadgets to create more time, more stuff packed into fewer hours—"You've got this," right? Well, guess what? You don't have to get this! Not by pushing yourself past your healthy, God-given boundaries. You don't have to get this because He's got this. When you reach the point of burnout, why not confess that soul-draining self-sufficiency? Just surrender. Lay it all out and ask the Lord how you should simplify—what to let go of and what to hold onto. Make time to care for one of His most precious creations: you!

It is not that we are competent in ourselves
to consider anything as coming from ourselves,
but our competence is from God.
II Corinthians 3:5 HCSB

But He said to me, "My grace is sufficient for you,
for power is perfected in weakness."
II Corinthians 12:9 HCSB

As often as possible Jesus withdrew to
out-of-the-way places for prayer.
Luke 5:16 THE MESSAGE

He is our God.
We are the people He watches over,
the flock under His care.
Psalm 95:7 NLT

Lord, I know I can't do it all,
and I'm sorry for the times when I try.
Help me to honor You by taking care of me.

AUTHENTIC LIFE

Are you a truth-teller? Not in the sense of telling a lie versus telling the truth. But how authentically do you share your life with others? Do you offer the G-rated version to ensure that no one knows you're an actual human being who struggles sometimes? Or do you share some of it but leave out the embarrassing parts because someone might think less of you? Here's a funny thing about truth-telling: being vulnerable in your interactions with others often has the opposite effect than what you'd expect: it disarms people and invites them to be honest about their own lives. Following Jesus requires slowing down long enough to pay attention to what's going on inside us and then being willing to share it—even with just one trusted friend. Don't be lured into telling the social-media version of your life. Be a pioneer for Christ-centered authenticity.

When the Spirit of truth comes,
He will guide you into all the truth.
John 16:13 HCSB

Therefore each of you must put off falsehood
and speak truthfully to your neighbor,
for we are all members of one body.
Ephesians 4:25 NIV

But His answer was: "My grace is all you need,
for My power is greatest when you are weak."
II Corinthians 12:9 GNT

For at one time you were darkness,
but now you are light in the Lord.
Walk as children of light.
Ephesians 5:8 ESV

PRAYER:

Lord, You know all the ways I try to hide
from You and others. Help me to live more authentically
in the light of Your love every day.

CHOOSE TO BLESS

Few things can zap our energy like anger and resentment. Whether it's a snarky social-media post, relentless rush-hour traffic, or a painful memory we can't seem to shake, bitterness can blindside us in a heartbeat. If unkind thoughts begin playing in your head, just remember: God's Word is a different soundtrack altogether, and you have a choice about what you're listening to! The next time frustration toward someone hits, take those thoughts captive. You can turn down the grumbles and turn up the grace. Speak these words aloud—even a whisper will do—while you hold that person in your heart: "The grace of the Lord Jesus Christ be with your spirit" (Philemon 1:25 NIV). Let the power of His Word set you free.

The Lord be with your spirit.
Grace be with you all.
II Timothy 4:22 NIV

We are taking every thought captive
to the obedience of Christ.
II Corinthians 10:5 NASB

Bless those who persecute you.
Don't curse them; pray that God will bless them.
Romans 12:14 NLT

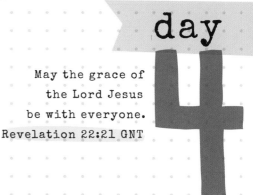

day 4

May the grace of
the Lord Jesus
be with everyone.
Revelation 22:21 GNT

PRAYER:

Lord, help me to let go of frustration
and speak Your words of truth into others' lives.
I want to be a vessel for Your grace.

JUST BE YOU

Do you ever marvel at how nature just does what it was created to do?

A bird selecting bits of your backyard fashions the perfect nest. The tree that holds that nest provides shelter and sustenance. Watching creation carry out God's work in the world is a beautiful thing to behold. And you, dear one, are part of creation, designed to share His love in ways that only you can. Be prayerful about the opportunities life brings. There will be things that obviously fit with your gifts and others that feel exhausting because you're just not cut out for them. That's perfectly okay! The Lord knows what makes you come alive, and when He calls you into something, you'll have a deep sense of its rightness for you. Just keep turning your heart toward Him and He will lead the way.

In his hand is the life of every living thing
and the breath of all mankind.
Job 12:10 ESV

When I consider Your heavens, the work of Your fingers, the moon
and the stars, which You have set in place, what is mankind that
You are mindful of them, human beings that You care for them?
Psalm 8:3–4 NIV

For You created my inmost being;
You knit me together in my mother's womb.
I praise you because I am fearfully and wonderfully made.
Psalm 139:13–14 NIV

day 5

Whether you turn to the right or to the left,
your ears will hear a voice behind you,
saying, "This is the way; walk in it."

Isaiah 30:21 NIV

PRAYER:

Lord, I'm in awe of all You have made!
Show me how You've created me to share
Your heart with the world.

PUT ON LOVE

It seems like we make a thousand choices every day...what to wear, what to eat, what to do, where to go, who to connect with.... Just thinking about it can be exhausting! Whether you're a dynamic decision maker or a professional procrastinator, there's no getting around it: these things won't figure themselves out. But there's one choice you can make the moment you wake up that puts all others in perspective. Make the decision to "put on love" (Colossians 3:14 NIV). Again and again. No matter what happens, it's one of the most important things you'll do today. Because, as Paul reminds us, we can do countless amazing, faith-filled things, but without love, we're nothing. It's tough to admit sometimes, because often the choice to love is way more difficult than the alternative. But it's always the right choice, and Jesus will always show us the way.

Love is more important than anything else.
It is what ties everything completely together.
Colossians 3:14 CEV

Do nothing out of rivalry or conceit,
but in humility consider others
as more important than yourselves.
Philippians 2:3 HCSB

Serve one another humbly in love.
Galatians 5:13 NIV

I give you a new command:
Love one another. Just as I have loved you,
you must also love one another.
John 13:34 HCSB

Lord, remind me every day to put on love.
No matter what decisions lie before me,
my heart is in Your hands.

ALL ABOUT THE JOURNEY

If you ever visit Maui, Hawaii, it's likely that someone will recommend to you the Road to Hana. It's a sixty-four-mile drive that begins on one side of the island and ends on the other. The trip is filled with breathtaking ocean views, unique bridges, and sparkling waterfalls. And what you realize when you reach the actual destination (which is kind of a hole in the wall) is that the Road to Hana is actually about the journey—not the place you end up. It's such a good reminder for we humans who, for whatever reason, can get so fixated on destinations in life that we totally miss the amazingness along the way. And it's not just scenery we're missing! It's the beautiful details and the unexpected gifts God has for our hearts. Slow down. Pay attention. Look for all the ways He reveals His love each day.

You lead me in the path of life;
I experience absolute joy in Your presence;
You always give me sheer delight.
Psalm 16:11 NET

May Yahweh bless you and protect you;
may Yahweh make His face shine on you and be gracious to you;
may Yahweh look with favor on you and give you peace.
Numbers 6:24-26 HCSB

He refreshes my soul.
He guides me along the right paths
for His name's sake.
Psalm 23:3 NIV

The priest told them, "Go in peace.
The Lord is watching over
the journey you are going on."
Judges 18:6 HCSB

PRAYER:

Lord, You make the journey of this life a beautiful adventure.
Slow me down to experience Your countless blessings along the way.

VESSEL FOR LOVE

Think of this: no one on earth can love another person exactly the way you can. Your way of loving comes from all the things that make you you—your background or life experiences, gifts, passions, circumstances, strengths, struggles, your unique relationship with your Creator and how you live it each day. Everything comes together beautifully to shape the one-of-a-kind vessel you are for Jesus' love in the world. Never let the voice of doubt creep in and tell you that you're not loving in the right way or not loving as much as someone else. It's not about striving to love better; it's about letting go of anything that stands in the way. His Word says, "Love must be sincere" (Romans 12:9 NIV). Without pretense. That means the more authentically you live, the more of His pure love you can give.

Be sincere in your love for others.
Romans 12:9 CEV

For we are His creation,
created in Christ Jesus for good works,
which God prepared ahead of time
so that we should walk in them.
Ephesians 2:10 HCSB

Yet LORD, You are our Father;
we are the clay, and You are our potter;
we all are the work of Your hands.
Isaiah 64:8 HCSB

Dear friends, let us love one another,
because love is from God,
and everyone who loves
has been born of God and knows God.
I John 4:7 HCSB

Lord, it's humbling to think that
You created me with such intention.
How are You calling me to share Your love today?

DARE TO DOWNSHIFT

Wouldn't it be amazing to find a soft spot, flop down, and just *be* every once in a while? To stop the chores and the calls and the calendar chaos and do nothing but breathe? Well, guess what? You can! But only if you choose to. Beware of the constant energy that propels you to do more, be more, fix more, achieve more—it doesn't own you. No one does but Christ alone, and His burden is light. You're the one who shifted into third gear in the first place, and you're the one who can put on the brakes any time you need. Don't fall for the lie that it all has to be done now, done perfectly, and done by you. You may do it all eventually (but, news flash—the world won't end if you don't).

Do you not know that your body is a temple
of the Holy Spirit within you, whom you have from God?
You are not your own, for you were bought with a price.
So glorify God in your body.
I Corinthians 6:19–20 ESV

Then, because so many people were coming
and going that they did not even have a chance to eat,
He said to them, "Come with me by yourselves
to a quiet place and get some rest."
Mark 6:31 NIV

Keep company with Me and
you'll learn to live freely and lightly.
Matthew 11:30 THE MESSAGE

In peace I will lie down and sleep,
for You alone, O Lord, will keep me safe.

Psalm 4:8 NLT

PRAYER:

Jesus, I carry so much that You never intended me to.
I need Your wisdom to make priorities
and Your grace to heal perfectionism.
Thank You for never giving up on me.

KNOWN AND LOVED

No one on this earth knows you like you do. No one knows every memory you hold, every thought you think, every dream you tuck away. No one feels that painful lump in your throat when you're fighting back tears, and no one knows exactly what it does to you when you hear a certain song or see a breathtaking sunset. No one on this earth knows. But the One who made this earth knows you from the inside out...delights in your particular, quirky laugh...feels all the joy that moves through you...sits with you in silence when you have no words...and hears exactly what you're saying with your heart. Find peace in that today, dear one. Especially if you're feeling disconnected, misunderstood, or underappreciated. You are known. Every little bit of you. And you are loved just exactly as you are.

I am the good shepherd;
I know my sheep and my sheep know Me.
John 10:14 NIV

O Lord, thou hast searched me, and known me.
Psalm 139:1 KJV

The LORD your God is with you, the Mighty Warrior who saves.
He will take great delight in you;
in His love He will no longer rebuke you,
but will rejoice over you with singing.
Zephaniah 3:17 NIV

I will be with you always,
even until the end of the world.
Matthew 28:20 CEV

It's an indescribable gift to be known
and loved by You, exactly as I am.
My heart is forever Yours, Lord Jesus.

COMING HOME

The next time you feel frazzled, rushed, or stressed, notice how shallow your breath has become. When you shift into overdrive, all your parts scramble to catch up. This is just one way your body shows you the truth about who you are—a human being with limits, dependent on her Maker for every breath. Too often, our fast-paced lives rob us of the joy of slowing down long enough to connect with our Creator and be at home in our bodies. But it's vital that we learn to turn our absence into presence. How else do we expect to meet with God? If not here and now, then when—and where? Return to the moment with a few deep breaths. Place your hand on your heart, and just come home to yourself. In doing so, you'll come home to His Spirit within you. Find peace in God's presence today.

But we have this treasure in jars of clay,
to show that the surpassing power belongs to God and not to us.
II Corinthians 4:7 ESV

In repentance and rest is your salvation,
in quietness and trust is your strength.
Isaiah 30:15 NIV

I will give them a heart to know Me, for I am the Lord;
and they will be My people, and I will be their God,
for they will return to Me with their whole heart.
Jeremiah 24:7 NASB

For He knows what we are made of,
remembering that we are dust.

Psalm 103:14 HCSB

PRAYER:

Jesus, when I'm feeling disconnected,
guide me home to my heart.
I know that I can always meet You there.

CONNECTED IN HIM

God's presence is the shortest distance between two hearts. Just think about that. When you miss someone who's here on earth or one who has gone home to heaven...when you wish you could be there to protect a child or comfort a grieving friend...you have a direct connection with them in the Spirit through prayer. It's a wonderful reminder for those of us who struggle with the desire to control and protect. It's a gift to those who deeply miss a loved one or one whose heart aches for someone who's hurting. The Healer, Protector, Comforter, and Lover of our souls is here with us and there with them, all at once, all the time. When you're feeling fearful or lonely or you're longing to reach out, just take a moment to hold that person in your heart. Become aware of God's presence connecting you, and rest deeply in that.

Have we not all one father?
Has not one God created us?
Malachi 2:10 NRSV

And let the peace of Christ rule in your hearts,
to which indeed you were called in one body.
Colossians 3:15 ESV

I will not leave you comfortless:
I will come to you.
John 14:18 KJV

And the peace of God,
which surpasses every thought,
will guard your hearts and
minds in Christ Jesus.
Philippians 4:7 HCSB

PRAYER:

Lord, it's so hard to feel far from the ones I love.
Thank You for connecting us,
heart to heart, in Your presence.

DARKNESS TO LIGHT

Picture yourself standing under an overcast sky. Suddenly the clouds break up, the sunshine peeks through, and you're bathed in light. But when that light appears, something else appears too: your shadow. It may be vague at first, but the brighter the sun shines, the more clearly the shadow is defined. This is what happens when the light of Christ shines into our lives. Our shadows become very clear. We see the hurtful things we're carrying, the harmful choices we're making, and the ugliness we've been hiding in our hearts. This may sound quite discouraging, but it's actually the best news ever! Jesus offers us freedom from those shadows, but we're the ones who must choose to let them go. Don't beat yourself up when something is revealed in you. Confess it, leave it behind, and let the light of His love lead you on.

Turn us again to Yourself, O God.
Make Your face shine down upon us.
Only then will we be saved.
Psalm 80:3 NLT

For thou art my lamp, O Lord:
and the Lord will lighten my darkness.
II Samuel 22:29 KJV

And when all things are brought out to the light,
then their true nature is clearly revealed.
Ephesians 5:13 GNT

Every good action and every perfect gift is from God.
These good gifts come down from
the Creator of the sun, moon, and stars,
who does not change like their shifting shadows.

James 1:17 NCV

PRAYER:

Jesus, I bring my whole self—shadows that are
known and unknown—into the light of Your presence.
Illuminate my heart with Your love today.

ALL YOUR HEART

He didn't say we'd find Him with all our head knowledge. Or with all our best tries. Or with all our beautifully written books on spirituality. He said, "You will seek Me and find Me when you seek Me with all your heart" (Jeremiah 29:13 NIV). This requires some risk, some surrender, and some willingness to be vulnerable in ways we never have before. It means admitting that we don't have all the answers—and even if we did, that's not how we'll ever come to know Him intimately. To seek with your heart is a full-on experience, not an exercise in theology. Of course it's vital to learn all we can about Him. But our understanding of Christ will only be illuminated to the degree that we learn to savor His presence and walk in His love.

If you look for Me wholeheartedly,
you will find Me.
Jeremiah 29:13 NLT

And walk in love,
as Christ loved us and gave himself up for us,
a fragrant offering and sacrifice to God.
Ephesians 5:2 ESV

But be doers of the word and not hearers only,
deceiving yourselves.
James 1:22 HCSB

day 1

He guides the humble in what is
right and teaches them His way.
Psalm 25:9 NIV

PRAYER:

I turn to You with all my heart, Lord Jesus.
I want to discover You in new ways, every day.

BEAUTIFUL YOU

Girl, you need some mirror time. Not "put-on-makeup" time or "rush-by-and-check-your-hair" time, but time to sit and gaze at that shining soul who's looking back at you. Look at those eyes of yours—there's a whole world in there! Your mouth, how it curves up at the edges when something lifts your heart. Are there some wrinkles? Your face is telling your story, and oh, what a story it is. That girl who is you—she is a marvelous creation on a journey with Jesus. She needs to know, every day, how deeply He loves her—just as she is. Can you see His beautiful creation in her reflection? Just stop for a moment and take it all in.

She is far more precious than jewels.
Proverbs 31:10 HCSB

God is within her, she will not fall;
God will help her at break of day.
Psalm 46:5 NIV

My heart is confident, God; I will sing;
I will sing praises with the whole of my being.
Psalm 108:1 HCSB

I have loved you with an everlasting love.
Jeremiah 31:3 HCSB

PRAYER:

Jesus, thank You for seeing the true beauty in me,
and for helping me to see it too. There's no one else
I'd rather take this journey with than You.

BELIEVE IN POSSIBILITY

When you walk outside and gaze into the distance, you know that the line where earth and sky meet isn't really a line. It's just the limit to what you can see. Horizons can be tricky—sometimes they beckon us to discover the unknown, but other times they make us feel like there's nothing beyond our line of sight. Your life on this earth will always have horizons. There'll be times when you're excited to see what's next and other times when you can't imagine that anything could possibly change. Maybe it's a season of stress, grief, depression, or a rocky relationship. All you see is tomorrow being the same as today. Jesus would remind you in those times that, yes, for you alone, it's impossible. But with God, all things are possible. Let every horizon remind you of this: where you see limits, He sees possibility.

Jesus looked at them intently and said,
"Humanly speaking, it is impossible.
But with God everything is possible."
Matthew 19:26 NLT

Immediately the father of the boy cried out,
"I do believe! Help my unbelief."
Mark 9:24 HCSB

I know that You can do anything and no
plan of Yours can be thwarted.
Job 42:2 HCSB

Now to Him who is able to do immeasurably more than all we ask or imagine, according to His power that is at work within us, to Him be glory in the church and in Christ Jesus throughout all generations, for ever and ever! Amen.

Ephesians 3:20-21 NIV

PRAYER:

I want to see my life more and more through Your eyes, Jesus. I trust You to reveal the hope in every horizon, and I praise You for the endless opportunities You provide.

GRATEFUL FOR IT ALL

Here's the thing about the grass being greener on the other side: it's just so exhausting to keep climbing that fence! There is So. Much. Amazingness right in front of you at any given moment—beauty to be found, joy to be lived, love to be shared. When you wish for another kind of life, you miss the miracle of this one! God has provided all you need for kingdom living, no matter what you have, who you know, what job you do, or any other thing the world uses to define you. It isn't the grass growing on either side that matters: it's the life of Christ growing inside you! The more you nurture that life, the more you forget those fences and just find yourself feeling grateful for it all.

Give thanks to the LORD, for He is good!
His faithful love endures forever.
Psalm 136:1 NLT

A heart at peace gives life to the body,
but envy rots the bones.
Proverbs 14:30 NIV

And this is the secret: Christ lives in you.
This gives you assurance of sharing His glory.
Colossians 1:27 NLT

Be thankful in all circumstances,
for this is God's will for you
who belong to Christ Jesus.
I Thessalonians 5:18 NLT

PRAYER:

Your blessings are countless, Lord!
Thank You for all You provide each day—
for me and for every person on this earth.

CHANGES AND CHOICES

Now hear this: if you quit something, it doesn't make you a quitter. It just makes you a woman who used her God-given ability to set some healthier boundaries. Maybe it's a job or a sport, a Bible study or a volunteer event. Maybe you've discovered that you have too much on your plate or the timing was wrong or there's a toxic relationship involved that needs time and space to heal. If you start feeling guilty for having to bow out, remember this: you're doing the best you can with what you have. Just keep your eyes on Jesus. Ask Him to lead the way. Trust Him for the courage to set boundaries and make changes. Remember: His eternal perspective looks nothing like your little timeline. Just take a step and remember that no matter what happens, you're never alone on the journey.

For the Spirit God gave us does not make us timid,
but gives us power, love and self-discipline.
II Timothy 1:7 NIV

For I am the Lord your God,
the one who takes hold of your right hand, who says to you,
"Don't be afraid, I am helping you."
Isaiah 41:13 NET

Trust GOD from the bottom of your heart;
don't try to figure out everything on your own.
Proverbs 3:5 THE MESSAGE

The LORD replied,
"My Presence will go with you,
and I will give you rest."
Exodus 33:14 NIV

PRAYER:

Lord, I receive Your grace as I struggle
with commitments and priorities. I trust You
to help me through all of life's transitions.

ALL IN HIS TIME

When you're thirsty, it's likely you'll drink from a glass of water, not an entire pitcher. A swig from something that big is a surefire way to get soaked. Little mouth, big spout: it's science! Experiencing God is very much the same. He has so much to reveal to you that it's impossible to comprehend. Some seasons of walking with Him feel slower and more mundane; others bring heart-filling, soul-freeing transformation. It's important to remember that less-spectacular times don't mean you're doing something wrong. The Lord knows you aren't able to take it all in at once. His offer of a glass instead of a pitcher is a tender way of sharing Himself with you in ways you can take in right now. True revelation can't be rushed, so take a load off. Just set your heart on Him, and all you need will be revealed in His time.

The Lord is good to those who wait for Him, to the person who seeks Him. It is good to wait quietly for deliverance from the Lord.
Lamentations 3:25-26 HCSB

For my thoughts are not your thoughts, neither are your ways my ways, declares the Lord. For as the heavens are higher than the earth, so are my ways higher than your ways and my thoughts than your thoughts.
Isaiah 55:8-9 ESV

Yet Lord, You are our Father; we are the clay, and You are our potter; we all are the work of Your hands.
Isaiah 64:8 HCSB

Trust in the Lord with all your heart,
and do not rely on your own understanding.
Proverbs 3:5 HCSB

PRAYER:

Lord, I know that You will reveal Yourself
to me in Your time and in Your way.
I want to love You more each day!

CAPTURING MOMENTS

Think of some of your most memorable moments—maybe times when you marveled at nature, witnessed a milestone, or shared laughter with loved ones. Sometimes you want so much to hold onto those moments that you scramble to capture a photo or video. But fumble with that device for too long and the opportunity passes. So goes the story of documenting our lives with pocket technology. We stand back to observe more and lose ourselves in the moment less. We forfeit the true experience of presence and the joy of connection. God gave us the gift of making memories for a reason. And while it's nice to have images to look back on, sometimes it's even better to fully live in those moments and capture them only in our hearts.

This is the day that the LORD has made;
let us rejoice and be glad in it.
Psalm 118:24 ESV

But Mary treasured up all these things
and pondered them in her heart.
Luke 2:19 NIV

Every good and perfect gift is from above.
James 1:17 NIV

You make known to me the path of life;
in your presence there is fullness of joy;
at your right hand are pleasures forevermore.

Psalm 16:11 ESV

PRAYER:

Help me savor the moments, Jesus.
Thank You for the gift of this one, beautiful life.

ALL OF YOU, ALL OF HIM

Do you think Martha was listening that day, as her sister sat at Jesus' feet? Did she catch a few things He said over clinking dishes and baking bread? Did she wish that she, too, could just drop everything and sit for a moment in His presence? You can do so, you know, and it is vital that you do! Step out of the busyness from time to time. Press pause on your to-do list, silence your phone, close your laptop, and sit with Jesus. Bring all of yourself to Jesus. Wait in stillness for Him to speak to your heart. One life-giving word from Him is worth a thousand tasks completed, goals accomplished, or promises made. In Christ, we "live and move and have our being" (Acts 17:28 NIV). Your life may be filled to the busy brim, but it's good to remember that everything begins and ends with Him.

But the Lord said to her, "My dear Martha,
you are worried and upset over all these details!
There is only one thing worth being concerned about.
Mary has discovered it, and it will not be taken away from her."
Luke 10:41-42 NLT

He says, "Stop your striving and recognize that I am God!"
Psalm 46:10 NET

Draw near to God,
and he will draw near to you.
James 4:8 ESV

I am the first and the last,
the beginning and the end.
Revelation 22:13 GNT

PRAYER:

Jesus, I offer You all of myself.
Remind me often that my life is hidden in You.

BREAKING THE ICE

Have you noticed how naturally children without "stranger danger" will connect with any random person? It's funny to hear a little voice speak up in a public place where everyone is supposed to be on their best behavior. "I like your shoes!" Or "You smell good!" Or "What's your name?" It shocks people out of their comfort zones, makes them smile, and just seems to take the edge off. Sure, that's because little kids are cute. But it's also because they aren't afraid to break the ice and acknowledge the existence of the human beings right beside them. What's stopping grown-ups from doing that more? We might be surprised at how receptive people are—and how quickly they warm up to a little conversation. It may take a bit of courage to reach out, but why not give it a try? You never know what connections God may have in store.

Have we not all one father?
Has not one God created us?
Malachi 2:10 NRSV

Therefore, accept one another,
just as Christ also accepted us to the glory of God.
Romans 15:7 NASB

Don't look out only for your own interests,
but take an interest in others, too.
Philippians 2:4 NLT

Your speech should always be gracious,
seasoned with salt, so that you may know
how you should answer each person.

Colossians 4:6 HCSB

We're all made in Your image, Lord.
Remind me of that, especially when I'm with people I don't know.
Give me the courage to build bridges.

ALWAYS ENOUGH

News flash: if your fridge is messy or your desk is cluttered, it doesn't mean that your life is a wreck. Don't let the voice of the enemy (or the voice in your head) make a few little things into a big, scary story. Remember, there are lots of pieces and parts to your life, and God holds every single one. Even those that may need a little cleaning out! Ask Him to help you create some space to breathe a little easier. If something's bugging you or weighing you down, take care of it—or make a note and let it go for now. Then shift your focus to all the great things you have done! Give yourself a break. You're doing the best you can with what you have, and that is always enough.

So now there is no condemnation for those
who belong to Christ Jesus.
Romans 8:1 NLT

In every situation take the shield of faith,
and with it you will be able to extinguish
all the flaming arrows of the evil one.
Ephesians 6:16 HCSB

Return to your rest, my soul,
for the LORD has been good to you.
Psalm 116:7 HCSB

My times are in Your hands.
Psalm 31:15 NIV

Because of You, Jesus, I am enough!
Please remind me of that when I try to do too much.
My life is in Your hands.

DO UNTO OTHERS

Do you like it when people take the time to ask you about yourself and truly listen for your answer? Do you dislike it when others look around like they're distracted while you're talking with them? Think of the things that you appreciate and the things you'd like to change about the way people treat you...and then apply that to your own actions. Jesus' call to do unto others as we'd have done to us is simple and straightforward. If you complain about something others do, then make a point to never do that. If you're blessed by something, then remember it and do likewise. Sometimes we make the Golden Rule more complicated than it is. Sure, there are big ways to bless others, but it's the little everyday interactions that can add up to mean the most.

Treat others just as you want to be treated.
Luke 6:31 CEV

And let us consider how to stir up one
another to love and good works.
Hebrews 10:24 ESV

Through love serve one another.
Galatians 5:13 ESV

Friend, don't go along with evil. Model the good.
The person who does good does God's work.
III John 1:11 THE MESSAGE

Don't let me complicate it, Lord.
Show me how to love well, every day.

ALONG THE WAY

If you're into golf, you know how to set your stance, go for that perfect swing, and hope for a glorious outcome. But there's always more going on than just the next hole. There's the beauty of the course. The camaraderie in the cart—encouraging teammates, unexpected laughter, and celebration when the underdog claims impossible victory. To sum it up: your golf game is about so much more than the destination of a little ball. It's the same with your life game. We all have goals, but if we become too singularly focused on our ideas of how life was supposed to happen, we miss all the unexpected things God provides along the way. Slow down. Look up once in a while; see the beauty around you and the people beside you. They are His good gifts, and they make the journey so worthwhile.

Two people are better off than one,
for they can help each other succeed.
Ecclesiastes 4:9 NLT

And God is able to bless you abundantly,
so that in all things at all times, having all that you need,
you will abound in every good work.
II Corinthians 9:8 NIV

Every good and perfect gift is from above,
coming down from the Father of the heavenly lights,
who does not change like shifting shadows.
James 1:17 NIV

We can make our plans,
but the LORD determines our steps.

Proverbs 16:9 NLT

PRAYER:

Lord, I see You in all You've made.
Thank You for the beauty of Your creation and the blessing
of friends to do life with. What an amazing journey it is!

CREATED FOR CONNECTION

Remember the saying about no man (or woman!) being an island? It's a tough one. We like having control over our little piece of the world, and who knows what will happen if we let others in? They might rock our boat and steal our sunshine. They might challenge us to change or hold up a mirror we don't want to look into. But they also might become lifelong friends who help us make unforgettable memories. We're all broken and beautiful, and that makes every relationship complex in its own way. But hiding from people because of the tough stuff will surely cause us to miss the amazing stuff God has given us to experience together. We were created for connection, and His vision for humanity is not a bunch of isolated island-dwellers, but a community of vibrant love.

How good and pleasant it is when God's
people live together in unity!
Psalm 133:1 NIV

As iron sharpens iron, so a friend sharpens a friend.
Proverbs 27:17 NLT

Dear friends, let us love one another, for love comes from
God. Everyone who loves has been born of God and knows God.
I John 4:7 NIV

May Your Kingdom come;
may Your will be done on earth
as it is in heaven.
Matthew 6:10 GNT

PRAYER:

Father, help me to connect more deeply and
more often with the people You've brought into my life.
May we work together to build Your kingdom here on earth.

LET IT BE

Are you sitting down? Because this is a tough one to hear. On the day God calls you home, it is highly unlikely that you'll have all your ducks in a row. Even if you die at age ninety-nine and have lived a long, fruitful life, there'll probably be something left undone. It might be an incomplete to-do list on the counter. A phone call or a bed you haven't made. Perhaps some things you've been praying for or wondering about—but you don't have any answers. The bottom line is, there will always be something in your life that's in-process. And that is 100 percent okay! Your job is just to show up, trust God for another day, and take a step in His direction. Everything else will fall into place in due time.

There is an occasion for everything,
and a time for every activity under heaven.
Ecclesiastes 3:1 HCSB

He says, "Stop your striving and recognize that I am God!"
Psalm 46:10 NET

The course of my life is in Your power.
Psalm 31:15 HCSB

But blessed is the one who trusts in the LORD,
whose confidence is in Him.
Jeremiah 17:7 NIV

PRAYER:

You know the number of my days, Lord.
Remind me of that when I get ahead of myself.
I trust You to lead me, one step at a time.

KEEP ENVY OUT

Envy is sneaky. It comes knocking as a harmless guest, but if we open the door, we'll discover that it's always a trap. First we admire something. Then we start wishing it were ours. And soon resentment moves in and makes itself at home. We start believing, "What I have isn't enough. Who I am isn't enough. My life isn't enough." But God's Word is clear that nothing could be further from the truth! He's provided all you have and created who you are with such loving detail. Can you rest in that the next time you feel the nudge to compare and complain? Turn your heart in that moment toward the countless blessings you've received. Take time to celebrate all God's gifts—those He's given to others and to you!

I will give thanks to You, Lord,
with all my heart.
Psalm 9:1 NIV

You took off your former way of life,
the old self that is corrupted by deceitful desires.
Ephesians 4:22 HCSB

So rid yourselves of all malice,
all deceit, hypocrisy, envy, and all slander.
I Peter 2:1 HCSB

Give thanks in everything.
I Thessalonians 5:18 HCSB

PRAYER:

You are a generous God! Forgive me when I take what
You've given for granted. I'm grateful for all You've
provided—for me, and for all the world.

FAITH OVER FEAR

God's Word reminds us over and over that we weren't made to live in fear. Fear of being alone: "Do not fear, for I am with you" (Isaiah 41:10 HCSB). Fear of those who would intend to harm us: "Don't be terrified or afraid of them" (Deuteronomy 31:6 HCSB). Fear of death: "Even when I go through the darkest valley, I fear no danger" (Psalm 23:4 HCSB). Fear of bad news: "His heart is confident, trusting in the LORD" (Psalm 112:7 HCSB). Fear of being unwanted or unloved: "Do not fear, for I have redeemed you; I have called you by your name; you are Mine" (Isaiah 43:1 HCSB). Just to name a few!

Fear can squash joy, cause sin, steal freedom, and destroy relationships. Whatever fear you may be facing today, take it to Jesus. He's able and willing to cast it out with His perfect love.

Say to those with fearful hearts, "Be strong,
and do not fear, for your God is coming to destroy
your enemies. He is coming to save you."
Isaiah 35:4 NLT

There is no fear in love,
but perfect love casts out fear.
I John 4:18 ESV

The LORD is my light and my salvation—
whom shall I fear?
The LORD is the stronghold of my life—
of whom shall I be afraid?
Psalm 27:1 NIV

When I am afraid,
I will put my trust in You.
Psalm 56:3 NASB

PRAYER:

Jesus, fear can't exist in the light of Your perfect love for me.
I confess to You the things I'm holding onto,
and I trust You to replace them with faith and freedom.

FEELING ALIVE

If you plan it right, you can insulate yourself from most of life's discomforts—feeling too wet, too hot, too cold, too achy...too much of anything! What would our ancestors think of our twenty-first-century bubble? When life brought extremes, they had no choice but to feel their way through. Sure, modern conveniences have their perks, but a certain amount of numbness comes with them. Same with our inner lives. There are countless ways to anesthetize yourself from feeling too deeply—food, drink, drugs, screens, busyness. But what you gain in numbness, you'll lose in joy. God designed you to feel! Your senses, your heart—they weren't given to you to control and manage. They were created to help you come alive in Christ! So when the tough stuff hits, take a moment to connect with Him first. You may discover new ways to move through life with your heart alive and free.

Guard your heart more than anything else,
because the source of your life flows from it.
Proverbs 4:23 GW

You surely know that your body is a temple where
the Holy Spirit lives. The Spirit is in you and is
a gift from God. You are no longer your own.
I Corinthians 6:19 CEV

It is for freedom that Christ has set us free.
Stand firm, then, and do not let yourselves
be burdened again by a yoke of slavery.
Galatians 5:1 NIV

Seek your happiness in the LORD,
and He will give you your heart's desire.

Psalm 37:4 GNT

PRAYER:

Lord, I'm tempted to avoid feeling sometimes. Life can
hurt! But I want with all my heart to live fully in You.
Show me how to make that decision, one day at a time.

ENJOY THE RIDE

You're at the racetrack. A green flag waves; engines rev; cars zoom forward, and then...they just drive in circles. What?! Someone with no idea what's going on might think: "Why are they in such a hurry? They're not even getting anywhere!" Sounds a lot like the world we live in. People going around and around, just trying to get ahead. But Jesus has some Good News for those who follow Him: we're free to get off that track! No more need for striving, comparing, or proving our worth. No more exhausting ourselves to gain more just because that's what everyone else is doing. God is doing a new thing—laying out a new road—and it's infinite. It's not about laps and victory; it's about love and discovery. We're free to get out of the rat race and learn to enjoy the ride!

Instruct those who are rich in the present age not to be arrogant or to set their hope on the uncertainty of wealth, but on God, who richly provides us with all things to enjoy.
I Timothy 6:17 HCSB

So I decided there is nothing better than to enjoy food and drink and to find satisfaction in work. Then I realized that these pleasures are from the hand of God.
Ecclesiastes 2:24 NLT

For am I now trying to win the favor of people, or God? Or am I striving to please people? If I were still trying to please people, I would not be a slave of Christ.
Galatians 1:10 HCSB

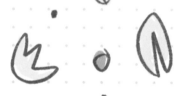
But God said to him, "You fool!
This very night you will have to give up your life;
then who will get all these things
you have kept for yourself?"
Luke 12:20 GNT

Praise You, Lord, for setting me free
from the endless cycle of striving.
In You, I have all I will ever need.

LET GOOD THOUGHTS GROW

Did you know that your natural mind has a default setting? It's like a negative vibe that hijacks your thoughts when you aren't resting in Christ. Don't believe it? Next time you're in a familiar funk, listen to what's playing in your head. It's most likely something untrue you once believed about yourself or the world. It can sneak back in and start dragging you down before you even have a clue. One of the most powerful, God-given abilities you have is to choose your own thoughts, because the seeds of your thoughts will grow into actions. The more you soak in His truth, the more fertile the soil will be for growing goodness in your mind. Weeds will crop up from time to time, but when you live in the presence of the Gardener, you can rest in His promises and leave the uprooting to Him.

Think about the things of heaven, not the things of earth.
Colossians 3:2 NLT

Whatever is true, whatever is noble, whatever is right, whatever is pure, whatever is lovely, whatever is admirable—if anything is excellent or praiseworthy—think about such things.
Philippians 4:8 NIV

We take captive every thought to make it obedient to Christ.
II Corinthians 10:5 NIV

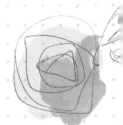

day

32

Do not conform to
the pattern of this world,
but be transformed by
the renewing of your mind.

Romans 12:2 NIV

PRAYER:

Fill my mind with Your truth, Jesus.
Uproot the lies, and replace them
with thoughts that bring peace and joy.

SIMPLE GESTURES

Sometimes a simple gesture of kindness goes further than we realize. Maybe it's helping someone carry something, speaking life-giving words to a discouraged friend, or offering a warm hello to a stranger. When we slow down long enough to meet a need, no matter how small it seems, we shine the light of Christ in our own little way. And while we have a limited view of those moments, God sees the far greater picture—what's happening in the Spirit. Every time we extend His grace and goodness, we help to grow His kingdom a little more on earth. Maybe one day when we reach our heavenly home, He'll allow us to see all the ways our humble gestures added up, one by one, to make an eternal difference.

And whatever you do, in word or in deed,
do everything in the name of the Lord Jesus,
giving thanks to God the Father through Him.
Colossians 3:17 HCSB

Your kingdom come.
Your will be done on earth as it is in heaven.
Matthew 6:10 HCSB

In the same way, let your good deeds shine out for all to see,
so that everyone will praise your heavenly Father.
Matthew 5:16 NLT

day 33

So let's not get tired of doing what is good.
At just the right time we will reap
a harvest of blessing if we don't give up.

Galatians 6:9 NLT

PRAYER:

Lord Jesus, show me how to
share Your love each day.

HIS CARED-FOR CREATION

Think of something your body does naturally—maybe your heart beating or your lungs filling with air. It's easy to take those things for granted, but they're actually part of the mind-blowing process of life, pulsing through you every day—a kind of symphony orchestrated by your Creator. He cares for the tiniest details of you and never misses a beat. Makes you wonder why you'd ever try to run things on your own. The One who spoke you into existence—who already "gets" you from the inside out—is with you in this moment, inviting you to trust in Him. What does that look like for you today? What small steps can you take into a life of greater freedom and joy?

She gave this name to the Lord who spoke to her:
"You are the God who sees me."
Genesis 16:13 NIV

Know that the Lord is God.
It is He who made us,
and we are His; we are His people,
the sheep of His pasture.
Psalm 100:3 NIV

For in Him we live and move and have our being.
Acts 17:28 NIV

You know me inside and out,
You know every bone in my body;
You know exactly how I was made, bit by bit,
how I was sculpted from nothing into something.

Psalm 139:15 THE MESSAGE

PRAYER:

Forgive me for the times I try to control everything.
You know me, Lord—every little part!
You're the One who holds my life in Your hands.

FOREVER CONNECTED

Your relationship with Jesus—do you ever find yourself taking it for granted? Sometimes you walk closely with Him and other times life's busyness leads you away. But His love toward you? It never, ever changes. And unlike some high-maintenance relationships, He meets you where you are, with compassion and understanding. No guilt trip about where you've been, no offhand comments about why you haven't called...just open arms awaiting your arrival. If you've struggled with connection lately, don't waste a moment feeling far from Him. Confess your lukewarm heart and receive His grace. Remember that you're always only one breath, one heartbeat, away from returning and resting in His love.

He will never leave you nor forsake you.
Deuteronomy 31:8 NIV

Live in Me. Make your home in Me just as I do in you.
John 15:4 THE MESSAGE

Your unfailing love, O Lord,
is as vast as the heavens;
Your faithfulness reaches beyond the clouds.
Psalm 36:5 NLT

Return to me,
and I will return to you,
says the LORD of hosts.
Malachi 3:7 ESV

PRAYER:

Jesus, Your heart for me is always open,
yet I so often fail to show my love. Whenever
my heart begins to wander, bring me back to You.

FREE TO LOVE

Making judgments can be exhausting, and we do it way more than we realize. From the smaller things ("She shouldn't wear that color") to the bigger things ("He should be living a different kind of life")—it takes heart space and emotional energy to fill a role we were never given. Jesus knew where judgment would lead us and reminded us more than once to leave it to God. The more we get tangled up in judging people, the less freedom we have to love them just as they are. We all live with our own brokenness and imperfection, but it doesn't define us, and it isn't ours to fix—it is Christ alone who will bring the darkness to light. Meanwhile, we can meet each other where we are, look for the good in one another, and trust God to take care of the rest.

How can you think of saying, "Friend, let me help
you get rid of that speck in your eye," when you
can't see past the log in your own eye?
Luke 6:42 NLT

So don't make judgments about anyone ahead of time—
before the Lord returns. For He will bring our darkest
secrets to light and will reveal our private motives.
I Corinthians 4:5 NLT

For God, who said, "Let light shine out of darkness," has
shone in our hearts to give the light of the knowledge
of the glory of God in the face of Jesus Christ.
II Corinthians 4:6 ESV

Be completely humble and gentle; be patient,
bearing with one another in love.

Ephesians 4:2 NIV

PRAYER:

Lord, I know it's not my job to judge others.
It's my privilege to love them! Remind me of this
beautiful truth when I'm tempted to do otherwise.

GET THE MESSAGE

Have you ever been to a restaurant where there are ten televisions playing and they're all showing something different? It's a little disorienting—you catch bits and pieces as you glance up now and then, but it's hard to know where to look! That's life today. We're bombarded with messages from everywhere. We struggle with what to focus on and who to believe. Often we don't have time to get the whole story, nor do we have the energy to piece it together. There are so many voices shouting and so few listening. Praise God for giving us His Word, an anchor of truth in a sea of uncertainty. The next time you're overwhelmed with info, just return to His simple message of Christ's redeeming love. It's the only story that will stand the test of time.

Just as the Father has loved Me,
I have also loved you; abide in My love.
John 15:9 NASB

Peace I leave with you; My peace I give you.
I do not give to you as the world gives.
Do not let your hearts be troubled and do not be afraid.
John 14:27 NIV

Don't copy the behavior and customs of this world, but
let God transform you into a new person by changing the
way you think. Then you will learn to know God's will
for you, which is good and pleasing and perfect.
Romans 12:2 NLT

day

37

You will keep in perfect peace
those whose minds are steadfast,
because they trust in You.

Isaiah 26:3 NIV

PRAYER:

Lord, it's overwhelming sometimes to be bombarded with
so many messages. But I know there's only one story that
matters—Yours! I'm forever grateful to have a place in it.

HE HOLDS EVERY SEASON

Spring, summer, fall, and winter. They remind us that all creation moves in rhythm—new life, growth, transition, and rest. The seasons of our lives have rhythm, too; some bring sadness and others, joy. There's an exchange of the comfortable and familiar for the new and undiscovered. We wish for some times to pass quickly, and we wish others would stay forever. But no matter what season you find yourself in, you can be sure of this: It is divinely woven into what came before it and what's coming after. Your Father provided all you needed to prepare you for this day, and right now He is growing in you the things you'll need for tomorrow. Hold this time with open hands and an open heart. Experience the beauty it brings, and allow yourself to grieve the losses. Everything will change, but His love will remain to see you through.

Everything on earth has its own time and its own season.
Ecclesiastes 3:1 CEV

So then, just as you received Christ Jesus as Lord, continue to live your lives in Him, rooted and built up in Him, strengthened in the faith as you were taught, and overflowing with thankfulness.
Colossians 2:6-7 NIV

You go before me and follow me.
You place Your hand of blessing on my head.
Psalm 139:5 NLT

My times are in Your hands.
Psalm 31:15 NIV

PRAYER:

Lord, I trust that You are working in every season of my life.
Thank You for going before me to prepare the way...
and for taking every step of the journey with me.

YES AND NO

How do you feel about saying no? "No, I don't have time." "No, I'm too tired." "No, I can't do that right now." Do those statements sound a little selfish to you? That tiny word "no" can be one of the hardest things to say because, for many people, it comes with baggage. When they hear a "no," they hear things like "I don't like you" or "You're not worth my time." But it is vital that we allow the Lord to redeem that word for us! "No" can be a space-creating, life-giving word that makes way for a great big "Yes!" in His time. Don't give little bits of your day away just because you feel guilty. Give your time with freedom and purpose! When you have to say no, let your answer be filled with gentleness and grace. God will do the rest. Just keep your eyes on Him.

Let your conversation be always full of grace,
seasoned with salt, so that
you may know how to answer everyone.
Colossians 4:6 NIV

I keep my eyes always on the LORD.
With Him at my right hand, I will not be shaken.
Psalm 16:8 NIV

All you need to say is simply "Yes" or "No";
anything beyond this comes from the evil one.
Matthew 5:37 NIV

For the Lord gives wisdom;
from His mouth come knowledge
and understanding.
Proverbs 2:6 NIV

PRAYER:

Jesus, I look to You for the courage
to say "no" when I need to and
"yes" when the time is right.

GOD'S WAYS

Kids (and kids at heart!) are fascinated by clouds, watching them change form, seeing characters take shape, guessing whether they hold a rainstorm. Clouds can be mysterious—we can see them, but we can't reach out and take hold of them. They seem so real and yet so ethereal at the same time. Isn't that how God's presence feels sometimes? He is so with you, and yet you just can't grasp everything about Him. You may reach out in faith, but you don't find what you expected. You get an idea of what He's up to, and then it changes shape and you have to let go of expectations. Remember this: The way He works in your life may be hard to understand sometimes, but His love? That's the thread that runs through it all. His love for you will never, ever change.

LORD, do not withhold Your compassion from me;
Your constant love and truth will always guard me.
Psalm 40:11 HCSB

O my people, trust in Him at all times.
Pour out your heart to Him, for God is our refuge.
Psalm 62:8 NLT

As you do not know the path of the wind,
or how the body is formed in a mother's womb,
so you cannot understand the work of God,
the Maker of all things.
Ecclesiastes 11:5 NIV

The steadfast love of the LORD never ceases;
his mercies never come to an end;
they are new every morning;
great is your faithfulness.
Lamentations 3:22-23 ESV

PRAYER:

Father, even when I don't understand Your ways,
I'll trust Your heart. You are always with me,
and I know Your love will never change.

JUNK-FREE LIVING

Junk mail. It's easy to spot in the pile. Colorful. Flashy. Makes big promises. But nine times out of ten, it ends up in the trash. Why? Because it doesn't take long to discover that there's not a lot of substance behind all the hoopla. If we do get sucked in, we'll likely end up thinking, "What a waste of time!" Well, guess what? The mailbox isn't the only place junk is sneaking into your life. There's plenty of it flying around, whether you see it on a screen, read it in a grocery-store aisle, or hear it from a human. You know instantly whether a message is worth your time. One of the gifts God has given us in Christ is a greater ability to discern light from darkness. Don't waste your headspace on empty promises, gossip, half-truths, and mean-spiritedness. God has created your heart for so much more.

In conclusion, my friends,
fill your minds with those things
that are good and that deserve praise:
things that are true, noble, right,
pure, lovely, and honorable.
Philippians 4:8 GNT

Gossip is so tasty—how we love to swallow it!
Proverbs 18:8 GNT

Look carefully then how you walk,
not as unwise but as wise.
Ephesians 5:15 ESV

Above all else, guard your heart,
for everything you do flows from it.

Proverbs 4:23 NIV

PRAYER:

Jesus, take the junk out of my life.
Give me the strength to step away from temptation,
and point me toward the light.

GIVE YOURSELF GRACE

Do you feel guilty for putting things off sometimes? "Maybe next year." It's tough when messages like "Seize the moment!" and "We aren't promised tomorrow!" are everywhere. Whether it's party planning, holiday decorating, or school volunteering, there's this pressure to do everything now and make it amazing. 'Cause maybe someone else always does. Or maybe you rocked it last year. But this time around? You just can't do One. More. Thing. And guess what? That's more than okay! The most important part of any gathering is God's presence, and you always have that! Sure, it's a blast to do it up big sometimes, but give yourself grace for those not-so-grandiose moments. You're a busy gal! Make Jesus a welcome guest, no matter what you're planning, and it's sure to be decorated with all you need—the beauty of His love.

Listen! I stand at the door and knock. If anyone hears My voice and opens the door, I will come in to him and have dinner with him, and he with Me.
Revelation 3:20 HCSB

And as they were saying these things, He Himself stood among them. He said to them, "Peace to you!"
Luke 24:36 HCSB

And whatever you do, in word or in deed, do everything in the name of the Lord Jesus, giving thanks to God the Father through Him.
Colossians 3:17 HCSB

My mind and my body may grow weak,
but God is my strength;
He is all I ever need.

Psalm 73:26 GNT

day
42

PRAYER:

Jesus, no matter what I plan,
You're the most important part. Please remind me of that
when I feel overwhelmed. All I need is Your presence.

HEAVEN IN YOUR HEART

Sometimes, if you slow down and sit quietly in God's presence long enough, you'll feel an ache that you just can't name. It's a little like homesickness or missing someone you love deeply, but it's so much more than that. And there's no earthly remedy for it, because it's a longing for eternal things. You were made for so much more than this time and space, and deep down, your spirit knows it's true. God has set eternity in your heart—a taste of your heavenly home—and it's just a glimmer of what is to come. Pay attention to that longing. Don't ignore it or try to satisfy it with lesser things. Draw near to Him and thank Him for preparing a place for you. You're on a journey to a glorious destination.

I heard a loud shout from the throne, saying,
"Look, God's home is now among His people! He will live with them,
and they will be His people. God Himself will be with them."
Revelation 21:3 NLT

If I go away and prepare a place for you,
I will come back and receive you to Myself,
so that where I am you may be also.
John 14:3 HCSB

He has also set eternity in the human heart;
yet no one can fathom what God has done
from beginning to end.
Ecclesiastes 3:11 NIV

You have been raised to life with Christ,
so set your hearts on the things
that are in heaven.
Colossians 3:1 GNT

PRAYER:

You created me for eternity, Lord.
I can barely comprehend it! Let the longing
I feel in this life draw me ever closer to You.

GREAT BIG LOVE

"Love you to the moon and back"—that saying is everywhere! We humans need big ways to illustrate the indescribable reality of love. Our Creator must smile on our sometimes-feeble attempts to understand it, and He must've known from the beginning how we'd struggle to share it. We have this biblical knack for wandering off the path of love and into the wilderness of self-centeredness. And just as God did for our ancestors, He helps us find our way back. Love isn't something we can drum up on our own, and we can't just dig down deeper for more. What we can do is trust Him to fill us up again. The biggest love in the universe isn't that moon-and-back love we celebrate on T-shirts and key chains. It's the eternal love found only in Him, available to us in every moment of the day.

Then I will give them a heart to know Me,
that I am the Lord; and they shall be My people,
and I will be their God,
for they shall return to Me with their whole heart.
Jeremiah 24:7 NKJV

You, Lord, are forgiving and good,
abounding in love to all who call to You.
Psalm 86:5 NIV

Beloved, let us love one another, for love is from God,
and whoever loves has been born of God and knows God.
I John 4:7 ESV

day

How precious is Your unfailing love, O God!

Psalm 36:7 NLT

PRAYER:

Lord, Your love is so much greater than I could ever imagine.
Open my heart to receive more of You each day.

LOVE, REFRESH, REPEAT

Be careful not to make people into projects. It's tough to admit, but sometimes that happens! Maybe it's a struggling coworker, a hurting friend, or a relative everyone tries to avoid. You've reached out to share God's love with them, but you find yourself spread so thin lately that they've become another item on your never-ending to-do list. Out of guilt, you call them or make one more coffee date, but your heart's just not in it. Remember this: If you catch yourself merely going through the motions, it's okay to take a step back. In fact, it may be the best thing for everyone. Let them know you're struggling too, and that you need some time to be refreshed in God's presence. Allow Him to pour into you, and trust Him to show you when the time is right to start pouring out again.

Don't just pretend to love others.
Really love them.
Romans 12:9 NLT

Remain in Me, and I will remain in you.
For a branch cannot produce fruit if it is severed from the vine,
and you cannot be fruitful unless you remain in Me.
John 15:4 NLT

Then Jesus said,
"Let's go off by ourselves to a quiet place
and rest awhile."
Mark 6:31 NLT

And God will generously provide all you need.
Then you will always have everything you need
and plenty left over to share with others.

II Corinthians 9:8 NLT

PRAYER:

Lord, fill me again and again with Your love, and I will share
it with the precious people You have brought into my life.

LAY IT DOWN

Pick up something small and chances are you won't have a problem carrying it around awhile. When our muscle fibers get depleted, they're naturally replaced by new ones, and life goes on. But pick up something heavy and it won't be long before you're straining big-time. The longer you carry it, the heavier it'll feel. That's exactly how emotional baggage works. You can tolerate the smaller stuff for a while, but the big things? Anger, guilt, fear, shame? You weren't designed to bear those burdens. And if you try, it won't be long before signs of struggle show up all over your life. You may be carrying something you picked up yesterday or years ago. Regardless, Jesus longs to lighten your load!

God, create a clean heart for me
and renew a steadfast spirit within me.
Psalm 51:10 HCSB

Search me, God, and know my heart;
test me and know my anxious thoughts.
Psalm 139:23 NIV

For My yoke is easy
and My burden is light.
Matthew 11:30 HCSB

You will know the truth,
and the truth will set you free.

John 8:32 HCSB

PRAYER:

Jesus, what am I carrying,
and how can I lay it down?
My heart is open to hearing Your voice.

JUST FOR TODAY

How often do you hear yourself saying the words "as soon as…"? "As soon as I get it right." "As soon as I have enough money." "As soon as I feel better." "As soon as I get some time off." Whatever you're hoping for is in the distance, and if you're honest with yourself, there's no guarantee that future day will come. Why not look around right now at the blessings that surround you—the things you aren't waiting for and the people God has given you today to love. Sure, there's a lot in process. That's life! There will always be something that needs to be bought or planned or fixed or finished. But there will also always be joys here in your midst—right under your nose—that God has provided for you in these moments. Don't miss them! All that "as soon as" stuff will fall into place, and if it doesn't, then you can trust that He has a better plan.

It is beautiful how God has done everything at the right time.
Ecclesiastes 3:11 GW

In any and all circumstances I have learned
the secret of being content.
Philippians 4:12 HCSB

I pray that God will take care of all your needs with the
wonderful blessings that come from Christ Jesus!
Philippians 4:19 CEV

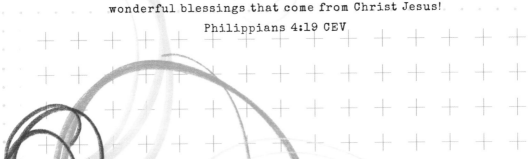

This day belongs to the Lord!
Let's celebrate and be glad today.
Psalm 118:24 CEV

PRAYER:

Lord, thank You for the gift of this day!
Open my eyes to the blessings right in front of me.

FRICTION-FREE

You and volcanoes have something in common. Surprised? Here's a little explanation: Volcanoes often form where parts of the earth are rubbing against each other. That friction creates magma, which in time makes its way to the surface and BOOM! You get the picture. You have friction in your life too—we all do! And wherever you find that friction, you'll find a potential source of anger and frustration. Where's yours? Maybe you're often saying "yes" when you really mean "no." Maybe you believe one way but you're living another. Maybe the clear vision you know God has given you is rubbing up against the fear of stepping into it. Wherever your hot spots are, it's vital to address them before things get ugly. Ask the Lord to reveal them and help you take steps toward change. Your future self will be so glad you did!

There is a way that seems right to a person,
but eventually it ends in death.
Proverbs 14:12 GW

Look deep into my heart, God,
and find out everything I am thinking.
Psalm 139:23 CEV

When the Spirit of Truth comes,
He will guide you into the full truth.
John 16:13 GW

TEN COMMANDMENTS

1. I am the Lord thy God, Thou shalt have no
2. Thou shalt not make unto thee any graven i
3. Thou shalt not take the name of the Lord

I have told you these things
so that in Me you may have peace.
John 16:33 NET

PRAYER:

Expose my hot spots, Jesus. It's a scary thing to ask,
but I know I need Your peace in those places the most.
Do Your revealing work of love in my heart today.

ds before me.

SHINING FOR HIM

Friendship with our sisters in Christ can be a haven in our sometimes chaotic lives. Our mutual love for Him and for each other is a vibrant picture of God's design for kingdom relationship—serving one another in love, speaking His truth to each other's hearts, being vulnerable in sharing our struggles and humble in sharing our victories, always being willing to bring our differences and disagreements into the light of His love.... What an opportunity we have to show His heart to the world by loving one another well. Our connection is like the clasp on a beautiful necklace—strong and secure, enabling the gems of His love to shine into the world in new and ever more beautiful ways.

For where two or three
are gathered together in My name,
I am there among them.
Matthew 18:20 HCSB

Serve one another in love.
Galatians 5:13 NLT

Make your light shine,
so that others will see the good you do
and will praise your Father in heaven.
Matthew 5:16 CEV

day

49

A cord of three strands
is not easily broken.
Ecclesiastes 4:12 HCSB

PRAYER:

My sisters in Christ are a priceless gift, Jesus.
Draw us closer to You every day,
and we will grow closer to one another.

LIGHTEN UP

Some studies suggest that four-year-olds laugh an average of three hundred times a day, but forty-year-olds? Less than ten! How about you? Proverbs 17:22 reminds us that "a cheerful heart is good medicine" (NIV), and that's evident in the lives of people who laugh a lot. Being with folks who emanate the joy of Jesus reminds us that it's okay (and even vital!) to celebrate life every chance we get. If you aren't one of those, what's stopping you? How can you help yourself lighten up a little today? Sure, we all have serious matters to tend to, but Jesus also invites us to let go of the worries of the world and become like little children. Childlike faith delights our hearts and makes life lighter. Give it a try. You may be surprised at how wonderful it feels.

He will yet fill your mouth with laughing,
and your lips with rejoicing.
Job 8:21 NKJV

You have put more joy in my heart than
they have when their grain and wine abound.
Psalm 4:7 ESV

A merry heart does good, like medicine,
but a broken spirit dries the bones.
Proverbs 17:22 NKJV

The LORD your God is in your midst,
a mighty one who will save;
he will rejoice over you with gladness;
he will quiet you by his love;
he will exult over you with loud singing.

Zephaniah 3:17 ESV

PRAYER:

Lord, it's hard sometimes to imagine that You,
the God of the universe, delight in me! Help me to let go,
lighten up, and share Your gift of laughter every day.

PRAY FIRST

See if this scenario sounds familiar. A problem arises, you get caught up in the moment, and you decide to grab the bull by the horns and solve that thing! You're smart; you're capable; this isn't your first rodeo. You know just what to do, and no one's gonna stop you! But in all your self-sufficient hoopla, you've missed one important detail: prayer.

Girl, always give yourself the gift of praying first. Your Maker sees much further down the road than you do, and there are likely some twists and turns you aren't aware of. Yes, He has absolutely given you the wisdom, intelligence, and experience to work through any challenge life brings. But you'll be missing out if you try to do it without Him. Take that first step of prayer, and then trust Him to guide you the rest of the way. You'll be so glad you did.

You can make many plans,
but the Lord's purpose will prevail.
Proverbs 19:21 NLT

If you wander off the road to the right or the left,
you will hear His voice behind you saying,
"Here is the road. Follow it."
Isaiah 30:21 GNT

Ask me and I will tell you remarkable secrets
you do not know about things to come.
Jeremiah 33:3 NLT

He said: The Lord is my rock,
my fortress,
and my deliverer.
II Samuel 22:2 HCSB

PRAYER:

Jesus, sometimes I get ahead. I forget that You see the path much more clearly than I do. I trust You will always lead me through.

OPEN YOUR EYES

Here's an eye-opening exercise. Walk through your house and find an unusual place to sit or stand. Maybe lie on the floor of the kitchen, or get crazy and climb (carefully!) onto a bedroom desk. See how different the room appears from that perspective. You're looking down at things you usually look up at—and vice versa. You see different angles and even new places to dust (ugh!). You might be inspired to rearrange a room or two! Friend, don't ever stop looking at life from new perspectives. Following Jesus doesn't mean that we all see things in the same way. Only you can see the world from your unique point of view. Life in Christ is multifaceted, offering new discoveries for each of us every day! The more you open yourself to Him, the more He'll show you new ways of seeing this wondrous world and all the precious souls you share it with.

Watch for the new thing I am going to do.
It is happening already—you can see it now!
Isaiah 43:19 GNT

Call to me and I will answer you,
and will tell you great and hidden things
that you have not known.
Jeremiah 33:3 ESV

Uncover my eyes so that I may see
the miraculous things in Your teachings.
Psalm 119:18 GW

How wonderful are the things the LORD does!
All who are delighted with them
want to understand them.

Psalm 111:2 GNT

PRAYER:

Open my eyes to new things, Lord,
in Your Word and in Your world.
Life in You is an endless discovery.
Help me to celebrate it every day.

RIPPLES AND REST

Ever thrown a rock into water and marveled at the ripple effect? As you watch the little waves move farther out, it's easy to miss the stone that started it all, sinking quietly to rest below. We're a lot like that ripple-making stone! God chooses us and sends us out to use our gifts to grow His kingdom. He calls us into seasons of doing—pouring ourselves out as vessels of His love. But He also gives us important seasons of being—coming to rest beneath the surface. It can be hard to slow down for those. We're created to live in rhythm—doing and being, motion and rest. Remember: Jesus made waves, but He also made time for stillness. It's important to know there's great purpose in both.

For we are God's handiwork,
created in Christ Jesus to do good works,
which God prepared in advance for us to do.
Ephesians 2:10 NIV

To everything there is a season,
a time for every purpose under heaven.
Ecclesiastes 3:1 NKJV

But Jesus would often go to some place
where He could be alone and pray.
Luke 5:16 CEV

On the seventh day
God had finished His work of creation,
so He rested from all His work.

Genesis 2:2 NLT

PRAYER:

Lord, may I find great purpose in work and rest,
just like You! Help me to embrace
each season of life as I follow Your lead.

WORN THIN

Do you have a favorite piece of clothing you can't imagine parting with? Something that's worn so thin, it's almost transparent? You love it not because it shows your flawless sense of style, but because of how soft it has become—feeling almost like a second skin. Life can wear us thin in some ways too. Things happen that make us feel more vulnerable, more exposed, rougher around the edges. We try hard to hide those parts—and wish we'd made better choices, used more wisdom, or found more balance. But guess what? Those very parts that make us feel the neediest are often the greatest entry points for God's grace in our lives. Because there's no pretense to hide behind anymore, we're exposed more intimately to His pure presence. When you're struggling, don't hide. He sees every part of you, knows you fully, and loves you as you are.

He said, "I heard the sound of You in the garden,
and I was afraid because I was naked;
so I hid myself."
Genesis 3:10 NASB

But whatever gain I had,
I counted as loss for the sake of Christ.
Philippians 3:7 ESV

I will not leave you comfortless:
I will come to you.
John 14:18 KJV

Now I know in part,
but then I will know fully,
as I am fully known.
I Corinthians 13:12 HCSB

Thank You, Lord, that in my moments of weakness,
Your gift of grace shines brightest.

LET IT SHINE

Ever walked into a house and been awed by the natural light surrounding you? Windows can make all the difference in the way a home feels. Through them, the hopeful morning sun streams in, warm spots of light appear on chilly afternoons, and the glow of evening invites us to rest and reflect. There's an illumination present that we can never replicate with human-made gadgets, no matter how hard we try. That's life in the Spirit. The more we open ourselves to God's illuminating work in the world, the more naturally our lives will shine with His beauty and grace. Striving to manufacture that goodness by ourselves is a waste of our precious time. We know the light doesn't begin with us—it shines through! So keep your curtains open and your windows clear. The people God brings into your life will be blessed by the light of His love.

For you were once darkness,
but now you are light in the Lord.
Ephesians 5:8 NIV

Make use of the Light while there is still time;
then you will become light bearers.
John 12:36 TLB

Again Jesus spoke to them, saying,
"I am the light of the world.
Whoever follows me will not walk in darkness,
but will have the light of life."
John 8:12 ESV

day 55

No one lights a lamp
and puts it under a basket,
but rather on a lampstand,
and it gives light for all
who are in the house.
Matthew 5:15 HCSB

PRAYER:

Shine through me, Lord! Make my life like a window
that helps others see Your illuminating love.

FROM THE INSIDE OUT

What do you want? Really. Do you even know sometimes? How often do you stop and listen to your heart voice—the one that's way deeper (and usually a lot quieter!) than your head voice? Do you really want to hurry to the next thing and the next thing the way you do? Do you really want that junky snack you just inhaled because there's never enough time? Overbusy lives often lead to mindless choices, because life on autopilot doesn't require a lot of deep decision making. But Jesus calls us again and again back to our hearts. Back to the reasons behind the things we do. Back to the "why" behind the "what." He knows that the only way to live full and vibrant lives is from the inside out. Stop once in a while and tune in. Your heart may have something important to say.

Delight yourself in the LORD;
and He will give you the desires of your heart.
Psalm 37:4 NASB

The purposes of a person's heart are deep waters,
but one who has insight draws them out.
Proverbs 20:5 NIV

Behold, You desire truth in the inward parts,
and in the hidden part You will make me to know wisdom.
Psalm 51:6 NKJV

For the word of God is alive and powerful.
It is sharper than the sharpest two-edged sword,
cutting between soul and spirit,
between joint and marrow.
It exposes our innermost thoughts and desires.

Hebrews 4:12 NLT

PRAYER:

Quiet my life, Lord, and help me hear what my
heart is trying to say. You alone know my deepest
desires. I place them all in Your loving hands.

LET HIM LEAD

You can always tell where God's Spirit is moving. Transformation happens; we start seeing in new ways; we loosen our grip on life-as-we-want-it-to-be and open our hands to life-as-He-is-creating-it-in-this-very-moment. That takes some hard-core trust, especially for those of us who have a hard time being vulnerable. Is it really possible that tomorrow can bring something we can't possibly imagine today? Will we pull back on the reins and dread the unknown, or will we take the leap and dance in the dark, trusting that His love will always light the path ahead? Our time on earth is short compared to the glory that's to come. So let the Spirit lead! In Christ, you have nothing to lose and everything to gain.

See, I am doing a new thing! Now it springs up;
do you not perceive it? I am making a way in the
wilderness and streams in the wasteland.
Isaiah 43:19 NIV

Now all glory to God, who is able,
through His mighty power at work within us,
to accomplish infinitely more than we might ask or think.
Ephesians 3:20 NLT

Now the Lord is the Spirit,
and where the Spirit of the Lord is,
there is freedom.
II Corinthians 3:17 NIV

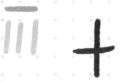

Trust in the LORD with all your heart
and do not lean on your own understanding.
In all your ways acknowledge Him,
and He will make your paths straight.
Proverbs 3:5-6 NASB

PRAYER:

O God, loosen my grip on my life and
draw me into greater freedom in Christ.
Fill me with Your Spirit in new ways every day!

THE CHOICE IS YOURS

How will you live this day? Will you notice the sunrise and marvel at the beauty of God's creation? Or will you wake up, check your phone, gulp some coffee, and switch to autopilot again? Will you dream of new adventures and pray for fresh revelation? Or will you settle into old patterns and complain that nothing ever changes? Will you brush past that person walking by on the street? Or will you honor their presence with a genuine, heartwarming smile? Will you look at the girl in the mirror and only notice the things you want to change about her? Or will you see the one-of-a-kind child of God you are? It's easy to forget that you're making these choices (and countless others!) every day. Slow down and take your life's journey with intention. You'll be amazed at the things you've been missing along the way.

Now listen! Today I am giving you
a choice between life and death,
between prosperity and disaster.
Deuteronomy 30:15 NLT

This is the day the Lord has made.
We will rejoice and be glad in it.
Psalm 118:24 NLT

Let all that you do be done in love.
I Corinthians 16:14 NASB

Slow down.
Take a deep breath.
What's the hurry?
Jeremiah 2:25 THE MESSAGE

PRAYER:

Jesus, I choose You, again and again.
I choose Your way of living the one, beautiful life
You've given me. Help me not to miss it!

ONE THING WELL

Are you a multitasker? It sure sounds like a great idea. Knocking two or three things off the list in record time? Yes, please! Maybe it's shopping online while cooking dinner, folding laundry, and somehow binge-watching your favorite shows all at once. Whatever kind of juggling you've got goin' on, it's probably pretty impressive. But did you know that our brains can't effectively switch between tasks after all? Studies have shown that we lose more time by making frequent mistakes, we don't retain as much, we become more forgetful, and our relationships can suffer. Seems we're wired by our Creator to do one thing well at a time. Why not try simplifying a bit? It may seem very uncomfortable at first, but you might find that you enjoy being more present and less scattered. Just ask the One who made you to show you where to start.

Do not conform to the pattern of this world,
but be transformed by the renewing of your mind.
Romans 12:2 NIV

Be very careful, then, how you live—
not as unwise but as wise.
Ephesians 5:15 NIV

I will instruct you and teach you in the way you should go;
I will counsel you with My loving eye on you.
Psalm 32:8 NIV

And whatever you do, whether in word or deed,
do it all in the name of the Lord Jesus,
giving thanks to God the Father through Him.
Colossians 3:17 NIV

PRAYER:

It's hard to imagine slowing down sometimes, Jesus,
but I know that all things are possible with You!
Help me to simplify and be present in all I do.

THE COMFORT OF CHRIST

One of the greatest ways You can share Christ with people in this crazy-busy world is to give them a soft place to land. You see someone who looks beaten down and recognize that look of exhaustion because you've been there (maybe you are there!). There might be tears right behind her smile or an old tape playing in his head that says he will never, ever measure up. You don't even need to know the details. You just need to feel the Spirit's nudge—extend your arms for a hug or ask, "Are you okay?" and wait for a genuine answer. Offer to help in some way or lift up a prayer for their peace. That's you doing what you were created for—simply being a vessel for the love of Jesus. May the Lord bring You opportunities to do so, and may others do the same for you when you need it most.

Praise the God and Father of our Lord Jesus Christ,
the Father of mercies and the God of all comfort.
II Corinthians 1:3 HCSB

We should all be concerned about our neighbor
and the good things that will build his faith.
Romans 15:2 GW

Whenever other people suffer,
we are able to comfort them by using the same comfort
we have received from God.
II Corinthians 1:4 GW

Do to others as you would like them to do to you.

Luke 6:31 NLT

PRAYER:

Lord, I want to be there for others
when life feels overwhelming. Make my heart
sensitive to the voice of Your Spirit.

STOP THAT LEAK

That dripping faucet. You know the one. It's midnight; you've tried everything—so you just give up and put something under it to catch the water. The next morning, you're astounded to find that container overflowing. This is a perfect picture of those nagging things in life that can overtake your heart. Someone repeatedly hurts your feelings, but instead of being honest with them, you just keep swallowing it. You see a coworker being mistreated, but you don't want to rock the boat, so you keep turning a blind eye. Maybe it's an energy-depleting friendship or a family member with zero respect for boundaries—whatever your thing is, it will spill over eventually if you don't fix that faucet now. Is there something filling you with frustration today? Search your heart and call on Jesus. He will give you exactly what you need to make a change.

Look deep into my heart, God,
and find out everything I am thinking.
Psalm 139:23 CEV

Watch over your heart with all diligence,
for from it flow the springs of life.
Proverbs 4:23 NASB

Get rid of all bitterness, rage and anger,
brawling and slander, along with every form of malice.
Be kind and compassionate to one another, forgiving
each other, just as in Christ God forgave you.
Ephesians 4:31-32 NIV

The beginning of strife is like letting out water,
so quit before the quarrel breaks out.

Proverbs 17:14 ESV

PRAYER:

What changes can I make in my life, Jesus?
I know I need to be honest about what's going on in my heart.
Please show me a step I can take.

JUST REACH OUT

There are countless ways to make a difference in this great big world. Technology provides a steady stream of opportunities and enables us to reach across the globe. However, seeing all the need all at once can be overwhelming. We can't help everyone, everywhere—but Jesus shows us that we can always help someone, somewhere (and that person may be right in front of us!). If you're feeling the weight of the world, why not take a moment to ask the Lord for one way you might open your hands and heart today? Whether it's someone in a far country or in the house next door, just take a simple step in their direction. You can trust God to meet you there with all you need to share His love.

And the King will answer them,
"I assure you: Whatever you did for one of the least
of these brothers of Mine, you did for Me."
Matthew 25:40 HCSB

Don't neglect to do what is good and to share,
for God is pleased with such sacrifices.
Hebrews 13:16 HCSB

We should keep on encouraging each other to be
thoughtful and to do helpful things.
Hebrews 10:24-25 CEV

For God is working in you,
giving you the desire and
the power to do what pleases Him.
Philippians 2:13 NLT

PRAYER:

There is so much need in Your world, Lord Jesus.
Show me where to start! Open my heart
to those who cross my path today.

TOGETHER AS ONE

Spend the night away from city lights and you may catch a glimpse of a soft white glow that stretches across the sky—the Milky Way. The funny thing is, it's our own galaxy we're looking at, from within. Stars, comets, asteroids, nebulae, planets—there are just so many, they seem to melt into each other. It's like the church. Not just your church or your particular country's church, but the whole church. The diverse family of believers on a journey with Jesus, being transformed into His likeness—just as you are—in their own unique way. You haven't met them all, and their lives may look different from yours, but you have one thing in common: Christ in you, the hope of glory. Take a moment now and then to celebrate this beautifully diverse family you're a part of. Honor your uniqueness and marvel at the ways He is bringing you together as one.

And this is the plan: At the right time He will bring
everything together under the authority of Christ—
everything in heaven and on earth.
Ephesians 1:10 NLT

How good and pleasant it is when God's
people live together in unity!
Psalm 133:1 NIV

After this I looked, and behold, a great multitude that no one
could number, from every nation, from all tribes and peoples
and languages, standing before the throne and before the Lamb,
clothed in white robes, with palm branches in their hands.
Revelation 7:9 ESV

One Lord, one faith, one baptism.

Ephesians 4:5 HCSB

Lord, what an indescribable gift it is to be a
part of Your family forever. Thank You for calling
each of us and bringing us together as one.

TIME TO LOVE

Overbusy lives can make deep love difficult. But that's hard to admit when we're living at light speed! God's call to "love each other deeply" requires slowing down and connecting heart to heart. Think of the ocean and all that's hidden in its depths—new forms of life we didn't know existed, treasures from long ago revealing ancient truths.... Deep waters offer endless discovery! Now imagine a tide pool—a few living things floating there, but not enough water to sustain life for long. When it comes to love, we have a choice: will we settle for the tide pool of our people, or will we take time to dive into their depths and discover all that God has created them to be?

Most important of all,
continue to show deep love for each other.
I Peter 4:8 NLT

For the entire law is fulfilled in one statement:
Love your neighbor as yourself.
Galatians 5:14 HCSB

We know that we have passed from death to life,
because we love each other.
I John 3:14 NIV

Love each other with genuine affection,
and take delight in honoring each other.
Romans 12:10 NLT

PRAYER:

Father, there's no limit to the depth of Your love.
May my life reflect that truth as I take the time to love others well.

MORE THAN BUSY

How often do you ask someone how they're doing and hear some sort of "busy" response? "Lots going on." "I'm swamped." "Can't wait till the weekend." Is one of those your default answer too? When you look at your life, is that really how you'd sum it up? Sure, you're busy, but aren't you also crazy blessed? And grateful? And a hundred other things? The words we speak matter—even the ones we say half-heartedly. One of the greatest ways to remind ourselves (and others) of God's goodness and grace in our lives is to say the words out loud. We don't have to deny a bad day or fake our feelings, but we can always find a hopeful response. The next time someone asks how you are, consider all the goodness. It will lift your heart and may just remind them that they, too, are way more than just busy.

Gracious words are like a honeycomb,
sweetness to the soul and health to the body.
Proverbs 16:24 ESV

And whatever you do or say,
do it as a representative of the Lord Jesus,
giving thanks through Him to God the Father.
Colossians 3:17 NLT

The tongue has the power of life and death,
and those who love it will eat its fruit.
Proverbs 18:21 NIV

So encourage each other
and give each other strength,
just as you are doing now.
I Thessalonians 5:11 NCV

PRAYER:

May my words bring Your goodness and grace into
the world, Lord. Before I give an automatic answer,
remind me to pause and choose to speak life!

THE GIFT OF PRESENCE

Studies show that Americans devote an average of ten hours a day to our screens. Whether or not this is true for you, it points to the reality that many people around you spend more time interacting with technology than humanity. Know what that means? Well, for one thing, it means you have a unique opportunity to show up for others in a way they may truly need. Simply offering your presence is a powerful way to share Christ in an increasingly disconnected world. Why not put down your own screen for a minute (or an hour!) and reach out in real time? Instead of checking e-mail in the store line, look up and share a genuine smile. Slip that phone into your pocket and be completely present with friends in conversation. Your willingness to be all there speaks volumes to others' hearts.

In the same way, let your light shine before others,
so that they may see your good works and give
glory to your Father who is in heaven.
Matthew 5:16 ESV

Let each of you look not only to his own interests,
but also to the interests of others.
Philippians 2:4 ESV

Therefore let us pursue the things which
make for peace and the things by
which one may edify another.
Romans 14:19 NKJV

Don't neglect to do what is good and to share,
for God is pleased with such sacrifices.

Hebrews 13:16 HCSB

PRAYER:

Father, show me the precious people
who need the gift of presence today.

TURN IT DOWN

Sensory overload—it's everywhere these days! Sometimes you just need a moment to think, but it's hijacked by a call or an e-mail or a late-breaking news story that sends you off on a tangent. Soon that quiet time you needed so much becomes a distant memory. And your tolerance for noise can grow so steadily that silence starts to feel strange. You might even find yourself avoiding it altogether! But it's hard to hear God's still, small voice when everything else is shouting at you. Remember: You are the gatekeeper for the noise in your life. You have the choice to turn down the radio, turn off the TV, silence the phone, close the laptop, shut the door. Give yourself that gift once in a while. You might be amazed at what you can hear.

Be still, and know that I am God.
Psalm 46:10 ESV

But the LORD is in His holy temple:
let everyone on earth be silent in His presence.
Habakkuk 2:20 HCSB

For God is not the author of confusion,
but of peace.
I Corinthians 14:33 KJV

After the earthquake there was a fire,
but the Lord was not in the fire.
And after the fire there was a voice,
a soft whisper.
I Kings 19:12 HCSB

PRAYER:

Help me to quiet the noise in my life more often, Lord.
I want to hear Your still, small voice in my heart.

THE JOY OF JESUS

Serious or playful? Which describes you more? Do you look for ways to make others (and yourself!) smile, finding humor when things gets tough? Or do you wonder how some people can seem so lighthearted and unconcerned about life? In Jesus, we see both sides: Someone who cares deeply about what matters, and Someone who knows how to lighten up and live joyfully. Yes, Jesus wept. But it's clear that He also celebrated, shared stories with a twinkle in His eye, and called us to become like the little children He took into His arms. We, too, can carry that sense of childlike trust through our days. If you feel out of balance, ask the Lord to help you see life more through His eyes—grounded in truth, walking with purpose, with a joy that makes your spirit shine!

A time to weep and a time to laugh;
a time to mourn and a time to dance.
Ecclesiastes 3:4 HCSB

You give him blessings forever;
You cheer him with joy in Your presence.
Psalm 21:6 CSB

Bring joy to Your servant's life,
because I turn to You, Lord.
Psalm 86:4 HCSB

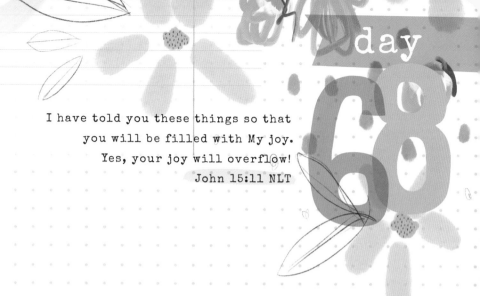

day

68

I have told you these things so that
you will be filled with My joy.
Yes, your joy will overflow!
John 15:11 NLT

Bless me, Jesus, with joy for the journey,
and help me to share it with those
You bring into my life.

LIFE IS GOOD

What would you say your default setting is—contentment or dissatisfaction? Do you have a general feeling of gratitude for the ways God blesses your life each day? Or do you find yourself wishing for different, better, more? Maybe it's a little of both! If you want to tip the scales more toward contentment, try hanging around with glass-half-full people. Their positive outlook and sense of gratitude for what is can rub off on you. They may not have much, but they don't wait to have more before they give thanks. They learn to look around and find the good things, right here, right now, and celebrate them. Try it for a day or two. Be like Paul and decide beforehand that life is good because...Jesus! You may just develop a habit that becomes a new way of looking at life.

Whatever happens,
keep thanking God because of Jesus Christ.
I Thessalonians 5:18 CEV

I will always praise the LORD.
Psalm 34:1 CEV

In any and every circumstance I have learned the
secret of contentment, whether I go satisfied
or hungry, have plenty or nothing.
Philippians 4:12 NET

Thanks be to God for His
indescribable gift!
II Corinthians 9:15 NIV

PRAYER:

Lord, surround me with grateful-hearted people.
Let the contentment I'm choosing today
become a way of life.

MORE THAN WORDS

Say you're sitting with someone, chatting over coffee. She says something, you say something, and then, suddenly... silence. What do you do? There's a theory that a pause in conversation happens naturally about every ten minutes. But some people feel so awkward that they hurry to fill the gap with words. What if the next time a convo falls silent, you sit back, take a breath, and honor it as a little window for the Holy Spirit to enter? If the other person feels the need to jump in, that's just fine. But you can enjoy a moment of rest in God's presence, savoring the company you're with and the relationship you share. Some of the most powerful connections we make can happen without words.

Let the words of my mouth and the meditation
of my heart be acceptable in Your sight,
O LORD, my rock and my Redeemer.
Psalm 19:14 NASB

My dear brothers and sisters, take note of this:
Everyone should be quick to listen,
slow to speak and slow to become angry.
James 1:19 NIV

Observe the people who always talk before they think—
even simpletons are better off than they are.
Proverbs 29:20 THE MESSAGE

day 70

In your presence
there is fullness of joy.
Psalm 16:11 ESV

PRAYER:

Bless my silence, Lord, just as You bless my words.
Let those in-between moments be filled
with Your beautiful presence. Amen.

UPS AND DOWNS

Rebounding, or jumping on a tiny trampoline, is a little exercise with big benefits. It's the upward and downward motions working together that make a difference in the body. That's our life in Christ! Both the ups and the downs together create the resilience we need to follow Him anywhere. Kingdom life can be heart-filling, giving us a taste of the joy God intended for us from the beginning. But it can also be heartbreaking as we live out His compassion for the world. There's so much beauty and so much brokenness that we can find ourselves "rebounding" between both. It's good to remember that God is allowing it to strengthen us and to expand our hearts as far as we're willing to let Him. Whether you're feeling the highs or the lows at the moment, remember that He's using every little thing for good.

Finally, let the mighty strength of the LORD make you strong.
Ephesians 6:10 CEV

We know that all things work together for the good of those who love God: those who are called according to His purpose.
Romans 8:28 HCSB

God blesses those who patiently endure testing and temptation. Afterward they will receive the crown of life that God has promised to those who love Him.
James 1:12 NLT

The LORD is my strength
and my shield;
my heart trusts in Him,
and He helps me.
Psalm 28:7 NIV

 PRAYER:

Jesus, You are with me through the ups and the downs,
and I'm so grateful to know that
You are using everything in my life for good.

THE WHOLE PICTURE

Say you're working a puzzle and you're so close to finishing, when suddenly...ugh! You realize you've lost a piece. You search everywhere, frustrated that your creation will never be complete. Now picture your life like that puzzle. There's so much to your story! So many circumstances and connections, experiences and emotions. From time to time it may feel as if a piece has gone missing—a lost relationship, a buried dream, a promise not yet fulfilled. The picture you imagined for yourself has a few gaps in it, and you're not sure how they'll ever be filled. But good news! Jesus knows just how everything will fall into place, sometimes in ways you least expect. If you're struggling with something, call on Him. The Bible says, "He is before all things, and in Him all things hold together" (Colossians 1:17 NIV). That includes you and every little detail of your life.

Christ existed before all things,
and in union with Him all things have their proper place.
Colossians 1:17 GNT

I alone know the plans I have for you,
plans to bring you prosperity and not disaster,
plans to bring about the future you hope for.
Jeremiah 29:11 GNT

And those who know Your name will put their trust in You,
for You, O Lord, have not forsaken those who seek You.
Psalm 9:10 NASB

My future is in Your hands.
Psalm 31:15 NLT

PRAYER:

Jesus, no matter how clear my life picture looks to me,
I trust You to complete it in Your time and in Your way.

LIVING WATER

Did you know that our bodies actually need water before we ever feel thirsty? We often walk around dehydrated because we don't get the "I'm parched!" signals our cells are sending out. We can function okay for a while, but soon things start to break down because, as we've all learned...water is life! And so it goes with our spirits. We know we need the living water Jesus provides, every day. But sometimes we settle for far less. Soon we find ourselves in survival mode—far from the vibrant lives we know we could be living. Just like the woman at the well, we don't know how thirsty we really are until we find ourselves in His presence. Sit awhile with Him today. Hear His words of life and drink deeply of His love.

Jesus answered,
"Everyone who drinks this water
will be thirsty again,
but whoever drinks the water
I give them will never thirst.
John 4:13-14 NIV

You will be like a garden that has much water,
like a spring that never runs dry.
Isaiah 58:11 NCV

You open your hand and satisfy
the desires of every living thing.
Psalm 145:16 NIV

day

73

And my God will supply every need
of yours according to his riches
in glory in Christ Jesus.
Philippians 4:19 ESV

I need You, Lord!
More than anything or anyone else in existence.
Draw me to Your well of living water every day.

WAKE UP

If you find yourself just going through the motions some days, here are a few simple ways to wake up: (1) Ask the Holy Spirit to show you a fresh perspective today and then keep your heart open for His leading. (2) Think of three things you take for granted and thank God for them. Maybe it's one of your senses or having clean water to drink or even just your next life-giving breath. (3) Do one new thing. Light a candle or turn on some music you don't usually listen to. Leave a few minutes early and take the scenic route to your daily destination. Try something different—a new flavor, new color, new experience—and savor it. Jesus is all about bringing you to life in new ways, every day. All you need is to be present, be grateful, and let Him lead the way.

And whatever you do, in word or deed,
do everything in the name of the Lord Jesus,
giving thanks to God the Father through Him.
Colossians 3:17 ESV

Clean the slate, God,
so we can start the day fresh!
Psalm 19:13 THE MESSAGE

This is why it is said: "Wake up, sleeper,
rise from the dead, and Christ will shine on you."
Ephesians 5:14 NIV

This day belongs to the LORD!
Let's celebrate and be glad today.
Psalm 118:24 CEV

PRAYER:

Wake me up, Lord!
You've filled my days with new joys and discoveries,
and I choose to open my eyes and my heart to them.

LOVE THROUGH YOU

Do you ever just need a hug? For someone to walk up, gather you in their arms, and hold you till every ounce of insecurity, doubt, and fear has drained away? There may be times in life when you're surrounded by people with plenty of love to go around. But there will be other times when the only arms available are yours. Want to know a secret? God's love can come to you through you. His warm embrace can be felt even when you're the only one in the room. The next time you're feeling alone and wishing for that healing touch, wrap your arms around yourself or put your hand over your heart and feel the compassion and kindness He's always pouring out. He'll provide other connections in His time, but don't forget that you, too, are a vessel for His life-giving love.

I am always aware of the LORD's presence;
He is near, and nothing can shake me.
Psalm 16:8 GNT

I will not leave you comfortless:
I will come to you.
John 14:18 KJV

But I have trusted in Your faithful love;
my heart will rejoice in Your deliverance.
Psalm 13:5 HCSB

Turn to me and be gracious to me,
for I am alone and afflicted.
Psalm 25:16 HCSB

PRAYER:

Jesus, when life feels lonely, fill me with Your love.

IN IT TOGETHER

When observing a road race, here are a few types of runners you're likely to see: The Gazelles: they lead the pack, trotting effortlessly toward the finish line. The Chatters: they plod along together, enjoying conversation and camaraderie. The Stragglers: they're out of breath after the first mile. But, hey, at least they showed up! No matter when they cross the finish line, something happens that brings runners together. They turn into encouragers. They see others pushing through to the end and know exactly how that feels. They may go back and join the cheering crowds at the curb or even run alongside the finishers for those last few exhausting steps. It's a picture of how we do kingdom life well. We run the race. We don't give up. We lift others up, and we never, ever struggle alone.

So speak encouraging words to one another.
Build up hope so you'll all be together in this,
no one left out, no one left behind.
I Thessalonians 5:11 THE MESSAGE

And I am certain that God, who began the good work
within you, will continue His work until it is finally
finished on the day when Christ Jesus returns.
Philippians 1:6 NLT

Your kingdom come.
Your will be done on earth as it is in heaven.
Matthew 6:10 HCSB

I have fought the good fight,
I have finished the race,
I have kept the faith.
II Timothy 4:7 HCSB

PRAYER:

I want to be an encourager, Jesus. I want to help bring
Your kingdom to earth in whatever way You call me to.

HE IS OUR PEACE

It's not that He helps us find peace somewhere or offers us His peace sometimes. It's this: He Himself is our peace. His presence equals perfect peace. And if His Spirit lives within you, that peace is already yours! When you find yourself frazzled, short-tempered, fearful, confused...simply stop and take a moment to turn your heart toward Him. Take your next breath in full awareness of His presence. Allow Him to remind you of His life-giving love. Let Him speak His promises to your heart again. The more you rest in who He is, the less overwhelming everything else becomes. Those problems that felt so big moments ago are put in their place in an instant. The path to peace is often much shorter than you think!

And the peace of God,
which transcends all understanding,
will guard your hearts and your minds in Christ Jesus.
Philippians 4:7 NIV

For Christ Himself is our way of peace.
Ephesians 2:14 TLB

But you have received the Holy Spirit,
and He lives within you, in your hearts.
I John 2:27 TLB

day

77

And He said,
"My presence shall go with you,
and I will give you rest."
Exodus 33:14 NASB

Your Spirit within me—what an indescribable gift!
May I walk in the peace of Your presence, Lord...today and always.

THE DOOR OF YOUR HEART

If you think about it, your heart is like a door; it can't be truly open and closed at the same time. It's one or the other, and you get to decide. Every day, in countless ways, Jesus invites you into openness. That's how you come to understand others deeply, to help their hearts feel safe in your presence, and to do your one-of-a-kind part in building the community of selfless love that is His kingdom. But beware of the forces that will try to slam that door closed daily. Fear, worry, judgment, comparison, resentment...the list goes on. Sin, in part, is a closing of your heart, and grace is an opening. The more you let go of those things that shut you down, the more freely you'll be able to give and receive God's limitless love.

Behold, I stand at the door and knock;
if anyone hears My voice and opens the door,
I will come in to him and will dine with him, and he with Me.
Revelation 3:20 NASB

Dear friends, let us love one another,
for love comes from God. Everyone who loves
has been born of God and knows God.
I John 4:7 NIV

The King will reply, "Truly I tell you,
whatever you did for one of the least of these
brothers and sisters of Mine, you did for Me."
Matthew 25:40 NIV

Above all else, guard your heart,
for everything you do flows from it.

Proverbs 4:23 NIV

PRAYER:

Jesus, my heart is Yours.
I want to keep it open to the world just like You do—
every day, in countless ways.

TAKE YOUR TIME

Do you ever wonder, "Where does the time go?!" The days fly by, but something deep within you knows that a clock doesn't hold the whole of your life. You were made for so much more! Ecclesiastes 3:11 reminds us that God has "set eternity in the human heart" (NIV). Yes, your earth time is limited, but your eternal time is...well...eternal! When Jesus came proclaiming the kingdom of God on earth, He brought with Him a new way to experience time. The more you step into the kingdom, the more you get to taste that eternal experience today. Let go of worry, marvel at creation, be fully present with others, see God everywhere. Every morning you wake up, you have a decision to make: will you rush mindlessly into this day, or will find ways to live in that glorious kingdom time? The choice is always yours.

He has planted eternity in the human heart,
but even so, people cannot see the whole scope
of God's work from beginning to end.
Ecclesiastes 3:11 NLT

For the kingdom of God is not a matter of eating and drinking,
but of righteousness, peace and joy in the Holy Spirit.
Romans 14:17 NIV

You will show me the way of life,
granting me the joy of Your presence and
the pleasures of living with You forever.
Psalm 16:11 NLT

Jesus Christ is the same
yesterday, today, and forever.
Hebrews 13:8 HCSB

PRAYER:

Lord, no matter what the clock says, I know that
You've given me a deeper way to experience time.
Draw me further into Your kingdom each day.

STORYTELLING

If you've ever listened to a dynamic storyteller, you know how riveting it can be. There's just something about the spoken word being shared with passion and purpose that inspires us and awakens our hearts. Storytelling has been around for as long as people have existed. It's easy to forget that before God's Word was ever written down, it was spoken! It's how we learned where we came from, where we're going, and how we gained the wisdom we need along the way. If you ever find yourself in a faith slump, one thing that can help lift your heart is to hear someone else talk about how God has worked in their life. It's good to be reminded of His faithfulness, especially when we feel doubtful and discouraged. Ask someone you know how God has shown up for them in a powerful way, and listen with your heart to their answer. You may be surprised at how quickly your faith can be restored.

For I am the LORD your God who takes hold of your right
hand and says to you, Do not fear; I will help you.
Isaiah 41:13 NIV

Therefore encourage one another and build each other up.
I Thessalonians 5:11 HCSB

Now faith is confidence in what we hope for
and assurance about what we do not see.
Hebrews 11:1 NIV

God is faithful, who has called you
into fellowship with His Son,
Jesus Christ our Lord.
I Corinthians 1:9 NIV

PRAYER:

Father, thank You for the gift of faith
and the power of words You've given us to share.

YOUR LIFE IS PRECIOUS

Consider this: Sometimes when you're overcome with anxiety or struggling with feelings of depression or wondering whether your chaotic life will ever feel "normal" again (whatever that is!), it's quite possible that you just need a really good night's sleep (or five), maybe a meal involving real food, or a little less time living in your own head and a lot more connection with others. It seems we humans have this ability to make mountains out of molehills when it comes to assessing the state of our lives. Yes, there are very real struggles that need medical attention, and thank the Lord for providing resources! But sometimes it's simply about our lack of self-care, and that's something we can choose to change anytime. If you're feeling burned out, consider some small steps you can take to nurture yourself. Give yourself permission to care for this one precious life God has given.

So He said to them, "Let's go to a place where
we can be alone to rest for a while."
Mark 6:31 GW

And the angel of the Lord came again
a second time and touched him and said,
"Arise and eat, for the journey is too great for you."
I Kings 19:7 ESV

It is vain for you to rise early, come home late,
and work so hard for your food.
Yes, He can provide for those
whom He loves even when they sleep.
Psalm 127:2 NET

You're my place of quiet retreat;
I wait for Your Word to renew me.
Psalm 119:114 THE MESSAGE

PRAYER:

How do I most need to care for myself now, Lord?
I need Your strength and grace to follow through.

WAITING WITH YOU

We humans aren't wild about uncertainty. We prefer answers and assurance, conclusions and closure. We don't like to be left wondering about things; it makes us feel vulnerable and reminds us how little we can really control. Think of a time when something in your life felt incomplete—even terribly unsettling. Maybe you were trying to locate a loved one to make sure they were safe or hoping for a job offer you thought would never come. Waiting is hard! Those in-between times can feel desperate, and you may be tempted to scramble and try to make something happen. But always take a moment first to turn your heart toward Jesus. His tenderness can be deeply felt in times of uncertainty. Remember that He is with you in the waiting—not just as a companion, but as the Creator who sees your life from beginning to end.

I am the LORD your God. I am holding your hand,
so don't be afraid. I am here to help you.
Isaiah 41:13 CEV

Brothers and sisters, as an example of patience in the face of
suffering, take the prophets who spoke in the name of the Lord.
As you know, we count as blessed those who have persevered.
James 5:10–11 NIV

Even when I walk through the darkest valley,
I will not be afraid, for You are close beside me.
Your rod and Your staff protect and comfort me.
Psalm 23:4 NLT

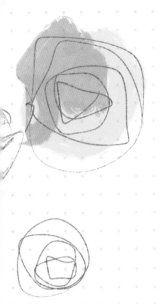

The LORD said,
"I will go with you
and give you peace."
Exodus 33:14 CEV

PRAYER:

Jesus, I want to feel how near You are
in my most unsettling moments. Thank You for
all the ways You calm my heart and bring me peace.

JUST SLOW DOWN

When did the fastest way become the best way? When did we decide that drive-throughs and microwaves, shortcuts and call-aheads would create a better life for us? Sure, time-savers can be helpful, but they've lured us into a quantity-over-quality mind-set. We squeeze five things into the amount of time we used to do one—and in the process, we lose the ability to enjoy any of them! Why not choose the slower option once in a while? Take a walk to the store, have a sit-down meal, go for the long phone conversation instead of a short text.... Experience the blessings that come from taking your time. You may even find that your Father has something to say; you've just been too rushed for too long to hear it.

Slow down. Take a deep breath.
What's the hurry?
Jeremiah 2:25 THE MESSAGE

Be still, and know that I am God.
Psalm 46:10 KJV

Everything on earth has its own time
and its own season.
Ecclesiastes 3:1 CEV

In their hearts humans plan their course,
but the LORD establishes their steps.
Proverbs 16:9 NIV

PRAYER:

Slow me down, Lord! There are so many ways
to savor this blessing-filled life You've given.
I praise You for every one.

PICTURE THIS

Close your eyes and think of a memorable time in your life. Maybe you stood in complete awe of God's creation or shed tears of joy for an answered prayer or laughed till you cried with a dear one. Can you see Someone else in that scene? Someone sharing your wonder, your celebration, and yes—your sidesplitting laughter? We may not see Jesus with our eyes, but we've been given a holy imagination to see Him with our hearts. Do you ever use it? We often associate imagining with pretending, but why not see it as a creative step of faith? Don't be afraid to go there, and trust God to help you see Him in new ways. Jesus was with you before you ever knew it, and He's with you in the moments you share today. Just imagine that!

For the Lord your God is living among you.
He is a mighty savior.
He will take delight in you with gladness.
With His love, He will calm all your fears.
He will rejoice over you with joyful songs.
Zephaniah 3:17 NLT

For now we see only a reflection as in a mirror;
then we shall see face to face. Now I know in part;
then I shall know fully, even as I am fully known.
I Corinthians 13:12 NIV

Look at me. I stand at the door. I knock.
If you hear me call and open the door,
I'll come right in and sit down to supper with you.
Revelation 3:20 THE MESSAGE

Give thanks to the LORD, for He is good;
His faithful love endures forever.

Psalm 107:1 HCSB

Jesus, You're there in every scene of my life,
even when I'm not aware. Open the eyes
of my heart to see You with me every day.

ROOTED AND RESTED

Trees do amazing things just by standing still—growing, blooming, changing with seasons, weathering storms with strength and flexibility.... How do they do it all? They're firmly rooted. From the beginning, as their visible part grew up and branched out, their unseen part reached down more deeply, creating a sure anchor for a vibrant life. That's your life in Christ! When you're "rooted and grounded in Him" (see Colossians 2:7), there's no need to strive for self-sufficiency. You don't have to dread life's changing seasons or try to dodge the inevitable storms that arise. You need only to be still and know that He is. He is your strength, your nurturer, your comforter, your protector, your bearer-of-burdens, and your calm in the chaos. Take a deep breath right where you are and remember how strongly you're anchored by His eternal, unfailing love.

This hope is a strong and
trustworthy anchor for our souls.
Hebrews 6:19 NLT

Let your roots grow down into Him,
and let your lives be built on Him.
Colossians 2:7 NLT

They will be like a tree planted by the water that sends
out its roots by the stream. It does not fear when heat
comes; its leaves are always green. It has no worries in
a year of drought and never fails to bear fruit.
Jeremiah 17:8 NIV

Christ in you, the hope of glory.
Colossians 1:27 HCSB

PRAYER:

Jesus, You are all I need!
Please remind me often just how near
You are and how secure I am
in Your everlasting love.

LOOKING UP

There's something big we've lost lately. Have you noticed it? Eye contact. Look around. How many people do you see in the store, on the street, or even at events who are actually looking up? Our screens have taken away the need (and often the desire) to acknowledge the person sitting next to us or the one we're passing on the street. Those little devices can connect us with what's going on halfway around the world, but they can't begin to replace the connections that really matter—the ones with people right in front of us. Sure, technology is amazing. But so is that shining soul behind the eyes of a stranger. Be someone who looks into those eyes. Offer a genuine smile. To acknowledge the existence of another human being is to honor the One who created us all in His beautiful image.

Then God said, "Let us make human beings
in our image, to be like us."
Genesis 1:26 NLT

So in everything, do to others what you would have them
do to you, for this sums up the Law and the Prophets.
Matthew 7:12 NIV

Therefore, I urge you, brothers and sisters, in view of God's
mercy, to offer your bodies as a living sacrifice, holy and
pleasing to God—this is your true and proper worship.
Romans 12:1 NIV

day 86

My command is this:
Love each other
as I have loved you.
John 15:12 NIV

PRAYER:

Father, wake me up to the shining souls
who cross my path. Give me the grace to be present
with them and to bless their lives with Your love.

OUR MARVELOUS MAKER

Nature reveals beautiful truths about our Creator; His fingerprints are everywhere! The heavens declare His glory, the skies proclaim His handiwork, the birds of the air and the lilies of the field remind us that He cares for every little detail of our lives. Taking time to reflect on the intricacies and the majesty of His creation can be a faith-builder. Just think—the One who fashioned every raindrop, placed every star, grew every towering tree from a tiny seed is the same One who knit you together and holds every one of your days in His hands. Make it a habit to simply marvel at His work. Look through the kitchen window each morning; step out the back door and gaze up at the night sky. Creation is like a love letter, revealing the Father's heart for the world. (And always remember—that includes you!)

My hands made the earth's foundations and spread
the heavens out. When I summon earth and sky,
they come at once and present themselves.
Isaiah 48:13 GNT

Great are the works of the LORD;
they are pondered by all who delight in them.
Psalm 111:2 NIV

Bring all who claim me as their God,
for I have made them for My glory.
It was I who created them.
Isaiah 43:7 NLT

God knew what He was doing from the very beginning.
He decided from the outset to shape the lives of those
who love Him along the same lines
as the life of His Son.
Romans 8:29 THE MESSAGE

PRAYER:

Heavenly Father, thank You for every detail
You've lovingly created. I want my life
to be a love letter written back to You.

WATCH FOR SIGNS

Think of the regular drive you take to a familiar place. When you get behind the wheel, you know that someone has laid out the road ahead, complete with all the stop signs you'll need for safe passage to your destination. Those signs are useless, though, if you decide to ignore them; they won't protect you if you refuse to slow down. Stop signs aren't nice suggestions; they're lifesavers. In the same way, when God commands Israel to take a Sabbath rest, He's not just saying that it would be a nice idea. He knows we're hardwired to need some stops in our lives, and He knows what happens when we ignore that need. Jesus rested, and you need to rest too. It's just the way you're created. Whatever that looks like for you, remember: it's not a luxury; it's a necessity!

I will always show you where to go.
I'll give you a full life in the emptiest of places—
firm muscles, strong bones. You'll be like a well-watered garden,
a gurgling spring that never runs dry.
Isaiah 58:11 THE MESSAGE

I will give those who are weary all they need.
Jeremiah 31:25 GW

He lets me lie down in green pastures;
He leads me beside quiet waters.
Psalm 23:2 HCSB

For He knows what we are made of,
remembering that we are dust.
Psalm 103:14 HCSB

PRAYER:

Running on empty isn't an option for me, Lord.
I know this, but how quickly I forget! Remind me often
to stop and just allow my heart to rest in You.

PAUSE FOR PEACE

Words can be so powerful, but sometimes the pause we offer between them is the most important thing. When someone says something hurtful to you or sends an e-mail that makes you cringe or a text that touches a nerve, what you do next can make all the difference in the world. These are the times when silence is, as they say, golden. Before reacting, before crafting that clever comeback, before raising your voice (OR TYPING IN ALL CAPS)...take a moment. Excuse yourself. Step away. Whatever you have to do to ask the Holy Spirit to breathe peace into your heart. Allow Him to guide your next steps and give you words of grace. They're more important than you may realize—for you and for those whose hearts will hear them.

What you say can preserve life or destroy it;
so you must accept the consequences of your words.
Proverbs 18:21 GNT

My child, find your source of strength
in the kindness of Christ Jesus.
II Timothy 2:1 GW

Now the Lord is the Spirit,
and where the Spirit of the Lord is,
there is freedom.
II Corinthians 3:17 NIV

Peace I leave with you;
My peace I give you.

John 14:27 NIV

PRAYER:

It's so hard to hold my tongue sometimes, Lord!
But I trust You to help me pause
and give grace when I want to snap back.
Bless my hardest conversations with Your peace.

LIGHTEN YOUR LOAD

How hard is it to admit these words? "I bought something, and it's no longer working for me." It's not broken, but it just isn't useful anymore. You face a dilemma: Will I let that thing sit around and hope it'll come in handy someday? Or will I lighten my load and let it go? Same goes with the rest of life—our attitudes, relationships, and commitments. Some things bring about God's best for us, and others are clearly dragging us down. There may have been a season for something, but it's past, and sometimes that's hard to admit. Check in from time to time, allowing the Lord to show you where He desires to bring greater freedom into your life by removing the things that weigh you down. You can always trust Him to know exactly what you need!

It is for freedom that Christ has set us free.
Stand firm, then, and do not let yourselves
be burdened again by a yoke of slavery.
Galatians 5:1 NIV

Test me, LORD, and try me,
examine my heart and my mind.
Psalm 26:2 NIV

Create in me a clean heart, O God,
and renew a steadfast spirit within me.
Psalm 51:10 NASB

There has never been the slightest doubt in my mind that the God who started this great work in you would keep at it and bring it to a flourishing finish on the very day Christ Jesus appears.

Philippians 1:6 THE MESSAGE

PRAYER:

Father, how would You lead me to lighten my load today? Please show me what I need to let go of, and help me to make it happen.

PROMISE TO PRAY

Are you an "out of sight, out of mind" type of person? If so, you're not alone. Most of us need little (or big!) reminders to help keep things on our radar—appointments, events, and meet-ups we've committed to. Do you ever think about prayer that way? If you've promised to pray for someone, you know how important it is to follow through. But it's also one more thing to remember in your sometimes overbusy life. Find some simple ways to keep those prayer requests front and center. Maybe a little list of names on the bathroom mirror or a kitchen bulletin board with small photos of each person or in this journal. Do whatever works for you, but know this: it's one thing to say "My thoughts and prayers are with you." It's another thing entirely to follow through with that promise every day.

I never stop giving thanks for you
as I remember you in my prayers.
Ephesians 1:16 HCSB

The earnest prayer of a righteous person
has great power and produces wonderful results.
James 5:16 NLT

Bear one another's burdens,
and so fulfill the law of Christ.
Galatians 6:2 ESV

Devote yourselves to prayer,
being watchful and thankful.
Colossians 4:2 NIV

PRAYER:

Jesus, I want to be faithful in prayer.
When I make a promise, help me do whatever
I need to do to follow through.

YOUR FORECAST

You're enjoying a beautiful day, when suddenly huge rainclouds start rolling in. You aren't surprised, because you saw the forecast and you knew a storm was brewing all along. In the same way, when your tired mind clouds over, you know it's just a matter of time before a struggle begins. Whether it's caused by stress, a lack of sleep, information overload, or just needing to put something decent in your body—a worn-out mind is fertile ground for discouraging thoughts. Two important reminders: (1) Be preventative! Take care of your inner weather. Do the things that create sunshine in your soul. Listen to your body when it tells you what it needs. (2) Find shelter. If a storm is brewing, you know where to go: Jesus! Let the truth of His Word outshine the clouds of doubt and fear. Rest in Him and remember that "He Himself is our peace" (Ephesians 2:14 NIV).

For Christ Himself has brought peace to us.
Ephesians 2:14 NLT

You are my hiding place; You will protect me from
trouble and surround me with songs of deliverance.
Psalm 32:7 NIV

The LORD is good, a stronghold in the day of trouble;
he knows those who take refuge in him.
Nahum 1:7 ESV

day 92

Those who live in the shelter
of the Most High will find rest
in the shadow of the Almighty.
Psalm 91:1 NLT

PRAYER:

Lord, renew my mind, and help me find rest in You.

BIRTHING SOMETHING NEW

Everyone knows that childbirth is no walk in the park, but it's one of those things we're willing to face because of the glorious outcome. Many women would probably welcome a pain-free, convenient alternative if the Lord provided one. But it is what it is, and the result is so worth the experience.

The same can be true of our spiritual lives. When God is birthing something new in us, it can be downright uncomfortable. We're likely to walk through some fear and insecurity as He calls us out onto the water. Letting go of the familiar can be disorienting, and given the choice, we'd probably run back or choose another way. But His ways are far greater, and He knows exactly what He's doing to bring us up in Christ. Just remember when you're there that the destination is so worth the journey, and He will never, ever let go of your hand.

For God has not given us a spirit of fear and timidity,
but of power, love, and self-discipline.
II Timothy 1:7 NLT

We know that God is always at work for the
good of everyone who loves Him.
Romans 8:28 CEV

I know what I'm doing. I have it all planned out—
plans to take care of you, not abandon you,
plans to give you the future you hope for.
Jeremiah 29:11 THE MESSAGE

"Come," He said.
Then Peter got down out of the boat,
walked on the water and came toward Jesus.

Matthew 14:29 NIV

PRAYER:

It's hard sometimes, Lord,
to understand what You're up to in my life. But I know
it's always for my good! Help me to trust in You.

TAKE A BREAK

You've probably seen stickers in car windows that show how many miles people have run: 26.2, 13.1 (or for the slackers, 0.0!). No matter how long road races are, most have one thing in common: water stops. And most runners would agree that those stops aren't just a nice idea: they're a necessity. Think about your own life for a moment. How often do you come to a place of feeling burnt-out and exhausted, only to realize how long it's been since you actually stopped to refuel? You know what they say: Life's a marathon; not a sprint. It's vital that you find moments of rest on the journey. Jesus did, and He desires to help you do the same.

The LORD will always lead you,
satisfy you in a parched land,
and strengthen your bones.
Isaiah 58:11 HCSB

Then My people will dwell in a peaceful
place, in safe and secure dwellings.
Isaiah 32:18 HCSB

Come to Me. Get away with Me and you'll recover your life.
I'll show you how to take a real rest.
Matthew 11:28 THE MESSAGE

But I have calmed and quieted my soul,
like a weaned child with its mother;
like a weaned child is my soul within me.
Psalm 131:2 ESV

PRAYER:

Jesus, You know how exhaustion feels,
and You know before I do when it's happening to me.
Remind me to stop now and then and rest deeply in Your love.

SURRENDER TO SLEEP

There's something special about nighttime. Do you feel it? When everyone's in bed, the world outside is hushed, and you're lying there in the quiet of your house...kind of like a caterpillar in a cocoon. The day may have been long, you may be exhausted, and your mind may be spinning with tomorrow's details and today's regrets. But whatever happens when you go horizontal, the quiet of nighttime invites you to peace. It's the perfect time to remember the promise of Jesus: "Peace I leave with you; my peace I give to you" (John 14:27 ESV). Let your spirit surrender to that truth every night. There may be countless conflicts happening in the world (some of them taking place in your own head!), but there is a peace that passes all understanding available for you to rest in right now.

God takes care of His own, even while they sleep.
Psalm 127:2 CEV

When you lie down, you will not be afraid;
you will lie down, and your sleep will be pleasant.
Proverbs 3:24 CSB

The Lord will send His faithful love by day;
His song will be with me in the night—
a prayer to the God of my life.
Psalm 42:8 HCSB

And the peace of God,
which surpasses all understanding,
will guard your hearts
and minds in Christ Jesus.
Philippians 4:7 CSB

PRAYER:

Lord, the quiet of nighttime is such a gift.
When I lie down, I'll rest in You.

FRIENDS FOR ALL TIME

Life brings some survival-mode seasons—the kind that require every bit of your energy just to get through the day. In those times, friendship may feel like it's on the back burner. You may feel guilty about having so little friend time or feel like your conversations are more about your own needs than theirs. But remember: In true friendship, there's no keeping track of who has done more for the other. If you walk together long enough, you'll see how the pendulum swings both ways. In some seasons you'll nurture friendships through loving service, and in other seasons you'll deepen them by resting in your own vulnerability and allowing others to bless you. When God's Word tells us "a friend loves at all times," it means all. While friendship may look different from day to day, it's a loyal love that can be lifelong.

Carry one another's burdens;
in this way you will fulfill the law of Christ.
Galatians 6:2 HCSB

Therefore encourage one another
and build each other up as you are already doing.
I Thessalonians 5:11 HCSB

For where two or three
are gathered together in My name,
I am there among them.
Matthew 18:20 HCSB

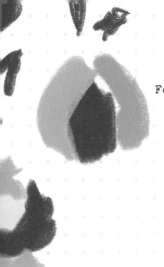

For everything there is a season,
a time for every activity
under heaven.
Ecclesiastes 3:1 NLT

PRAYER:

I praise You for the gift of friendship, Jesus.
Show me how to give and receive with grace.

LOOK INSIDE

Think of someone who annoys you. Maybe it's someone you try to avoid in the hallway or dodge at the holidays. What is it about them that makes you cringe? Did you know it's possible that person has something to show you about yourself? Your frustrations with others are often reflections of what's going on inside you. There may be something you try to hide (even from yourself!) and when you see it in another person, it's like an unwanted mirror. As usual, Jesus is the One who can see what's happening in the depths of you. He'll challenge your judgments and expose your true motives. Why? Because He loves you too much to let you bear the burden of hypocrisy. The next time someone gets on your nerves, check in to see if there's something more going on. You may just find the Lord has something to teach you through it all.

Don't be impressed with yourself. Don't compare yourself
with others. Each of you must take responsibility for
doing the creative best you can with your own life.
Galatians 6:4–5 THE MESSAGE

For everything that is hidden
will eventually be brought into the open,
and every secret will be brought to light.
Mark 4:22 NLT

If you need wisdom, ask our generous God,
and He will give it to you.
James 1:5 NLT

But the wisdom from above is first pure,
then peace-loving, gentle, compliant,
full of mercy and good fruits,
without favoritism and hypocrisy.

James 3:17 HCSB

PRAYER:

I don't want to hide things, Lord.
I know You can see the deepest part of me,
and I trust You to bring any darkness to light.

RENEWAL AND REST

Want to hear something scandalous? It's okay to take a day for yourself. Does this sound selfish? Irresponsible? Impossible? For some, it's hard to imagine an hour to ourselves, let alone twenty-four! But no matter what responsibilities you hold right now—work, school, family, volunteering, caregiving—it's vital to step away for some time to rest and allow the Lord to renew your perspective. Remember, renewal looks different for everyone—we're all uniquely designed! And if a day isn't right for you, consider setting aside a morning or an afternoon. Ask the Holy Spirit to guide you as you make a plan. Let go of the guilt, add a big heart to your calendar on that date, and remind yourself: "This is a day I'll pause to soak in God's love."

This is what the Lord says:
Stand by the roadways and look.
Ask about the ancient paths:
Which is the way to what is good?
Then take it and find rest for yourselves.
Jeremiah 6:16 HCSB

He gives power to the tired and worn out,
and strength to the weak.
Isaiah 40:29 TLB

Whoever dwells in the shelter of the Most High
will rest in the shadow of the Almighty.
Psalm 91:1 NIV

TEN COMMANDMENTS
I am the Lord thy God, Thou shalt have no other gods before
Thou shalt not make unto thee any graven image.
Thou shalt not take the name of the Lord thy God in vain.
Remember the Sabbath Day to keep it holy.
Honor thy father and thy mother.
Thou shalt

day

98

Return to your rest, my soul,
for the Lord has been good to you.
Psalm 116:7 HCSB

PRAYER:

I need time to rest in You, Lord, and You know just how
to make that happen. Help me to make a special date with You.
I trust You to know what's best!

YOUR PATH

There are countless paths your life might've taken, but this is the one you're on today. It's the result of your circumstances, choices, and connections—all unfolding under the umbrella of God's loving care. Whether you're happy about it or wish you'd done something differently, the truth is, you are where you are—and the way you choose to experience today makes all the difference in the world. A huge obstacle to resting in God's presence right now is being caught up in what "shoulda, woulda, coulda" happened, but didn't. Past regrets can steal your joy and take your eyes off the good gifts right in front of you. There's nothing wrong with a glance in the rearview mirror, but learn from what you see and let it go. Remember: when you're walking with Jesus, today is the greatest adventure.

Seek His will in all you do,
and He will show you which path to take.
Proverbs 3:6 NLT

You make known to me the path of life;
You will fill me with joy in Your presence.
Psalm 16:11 NIV

The LORD makes firm the steps
of the one who delights in Him.
Psalm 37:23 NIV

Your word is a lamp to guide
my feet and a light for my path.
Psalm 119:105 NLT

PRAYER:

The best part of this journey is walking with You,
Jesus. Help me to learn from the past, savor the
present, and look to the future with joy.

ONE OF A KIND

This moment that you are reading these words will never come again. This breath you're taking, this day you're rushing through—it is happening once in an eternity. Yes, it is just one tiny thread in the infinite tapestry your Creator is weaving together, but it matters just as much as every other part of that design. Look around you! Life is unfolding in countless ways right before your eyes, and you're being invited into it every day. "The kingdom of God is within you," says Jesus (Luke 17:21 GW). How can you bring that kingdom life into the world, right here and right now? He's calling you into joy and freedom and vibrant, wholehearted living. How will you respond on this one-of-a-kind day in your life?

Each day is God's gift.
Ecclesiastes 9:9 THE MESSAGE

I tell you, now is the time of God's favor,
now is the day of salvation.
II Corinthians 6:2 NIV

This day belongs to the LORD!
Let's celebrate and be glad today.
Psalm 118:24 CEV

I will thank the LORD with all my heart;
I will declare all Your wondrous works.

Psalm 9:1 CSB

PRAYER:

Thank You for this day, Lord—and for this life
You've given me. It is a precious gift,
and I want to live it with purpose and joy.

About the Author

Shanna Noel lives in Washington State with her husband of eighteen years, Jonathan, and their two daughters, Jaden and Addison. When they aren't covered in paint and Bible journaling, they are working on reclaimed projects around the house or catching up on the latest movie.

Shanna is the founder and owner of *Illustrated Faith* and the Bible-journaling community, and stands in awe at what God is doing in their creative community!

Also Available Books

Available at **dayspring.com**
as well as several retail stores near you.

Journals

More Resources

Bible journaling has become a tremendously
popular new way to connect with Scripture
in a creative way by combining faith and art.
To learn more about the Bible Journaling movement,
visit **dayspring.com/biblejournaling** today!